JOB EVALUATION

A PRACTICAL GUIDE FOR MANAGERS

JOB EVALUATION

A PRACTICAL GUIDE FOR MANAGERS

Published by Management Publications Limited
for the British Institute of Management

Published by Management Publications Limited
Gillow House 5 Winsley Street London W 1
for the British Institute of Management

© Management Publications Limited, 1970
First published 1970
Reprinted 1971

SBN 851 18066 3

Reprinted in Great Britain by Lewis Reprints Limited
Port Talbot, Glamorgan

CONTENTS

v

PREFACE

It is almost twenty years since the British Institute of Management published its first booklet on job evaluation. Since then, more and more companies have introduced job evaluation and there has been a considerable increase in the types of schemes used, some of which are highly sophisticated. This new book, entirely updated and including much new material, can be highly recommended as a clear, practical introduction to a subject which may seem complicated for those without prior knowledge or experience of its implications.

In recommending this book I wish to thank the writers' panel for all the hard work which has gone into its preparation. There is no doubt that their efforts will be warmly appreciated by those who read this constructive publication.

JOHN MARSH, CBE
Director General
British Institute of Management

ACKNOWLEDGMENTS

In 1952 the British Institute of Management published *Job Evaluation: a Practical Guide* which proved to be a very popular booklet. However, with the increasing interest in job evaluation and the development of some methods which were not dealt with in that publication, a need has been felt for a completely revised and extended edition. In February 1968 a panel was formed under the Chairmanship of Mrs A. L. T. Taylor and in consequence *Job Evaluation—A Practical Guide for Managers* has been produced. This is intended to serve as a broad introduction and explanation for those without prior knowledge and experience of job evaluation.

The British Institute of Management wishes to express its gratitude to the following members of the Panel:

Chairman: Mrs A. L. T. Taylor	— Urwick, Orr & Partners Ltd
Mr W. T. Aird	— British Broadcasting Corporation
Mr. R. F. Brown	— Massey-Ferguson Manufacturing Co. Ltd
Mr A. S. Harris	— Kodak Ltd
Mr T. A. Hindle	— Bowyers (Wiltshire) Ltd (formerly of the National Board for Prices and Incomes)
Mr P. W. A. Petty	— Beecham Group Ltd
Secretary: Mr E. J. Singer	— Urwick, Orr & Partners Ltd
Miss S. W. Aylett	— BIM Representative and Co-ordinator

In addition, Mr P. Fisher, of the Trades Union Congress, Mr E. Goldring, of the Glacier Institute of Management, and Mr S. Meredeen, of Ford of Britain Ltd, served on the Panel for a period and made important contributions. The BIM records its thanks equally to them.

The Institute also acknowledges its warm appreciation of help received from many other organisations and individuals who have assisted in the work of the Panel.

It is through the efforts of all the above that this new and updated manual on job evaluation is now published.

ix

FOREWORD

Job evaluation as a management technique has been employed by firms in this country and abroad for many years. However, the use of job evaluation is by no means universally adopted in this country. This publication is directed at those firms, which are ever increasing in number, that want to consider adding job evaluation to their management skills.

Sound management requires not merely the adoption of new techniques but rather the wise tailoring of management methods to the individual circumstances of the organisation. Job evaluation, like any other management tool, requires careful consideration of the circumstances in which it is to be employed, and a clear definition of what it is intended to accomplish. This is necessary before any detailed study of job evaluation techniques is required.

As there are now many books and publications on the subject of job evaluation, this guide is not attempting to add to the list of comprehensive expositions on one or more techniques of job evaluation. Rather the intention is to introduce the subject in the broadest possible way and to point out the main areas where analysis and decision making are required in the process of adapting job evaluation to a particular requirement. The reader who wishes to study specific aspects of the subject in more detail is directed through the Reading List to works which should be helpful in giving him a degree of expertise that this book does not pretend to provide.

Like many other management techniques, job evaluation has acquired a certain amount of mystique, created largely by the jargon employed by its practitioners. With job evaluation, as with critical path scheduling or data processing, the uninitiated must first learn the language. The language problem in job evaluation is compounded by the fact that even its practitioners do not always use the terminology in exactly the same way. With this in mind, the authors of this book have agreed to a set of definitions based upon the most common usage in the field. These appear in the Glossary. Care has been taken to ensure the consistent use of these terms throughout the book, and the reader is strongly advised to become thoroughly familiar with the definitions of these terms right from the outset.

CHAPTER I

AN INTRODUCTION TO JOB EVALUATION

Job evaluation is the process of analysing and assessing the content of jobs, in order to place them in an acceptable rank order which can then be used as a basis for a remuneration system. Job evaluation, therefore, is simply a technique designed to assist in the development of new pay structures by defining relativities between jobs on a consistent and systematic basis. This contrasts sharply with the practice in many organisations of making arbitrary judgments often based on short-term expediency about the payment of particular jobs, with no reference to common criteria and inadequate reference to the effect of pay decisions on other jobs within the organisation. The development of sound pay structures is more likely to be achieved using job evaluation than 'rule of thumb' methods.

Before defining job evaluation further and evaluating its utility to an organisation, it is necessary to differentiate between the various components usually found in total remuneration.

Components of a Pay Structure
The total remuneration of hourly paid workers often consists of many differing payment elements—base rates, plus rates, incentive bonuses, lieu bonuses, dirt money, tool money, shift allowances, long service pay, merit pay, and so on. The same is true of the managerial level where individuals often receive other benefits besides a basic salary, such as bonuses of varying types, a variety of personal and job allowances, supplementary pensions, car allowances, etc. It is useful to categorise these elements and see them as relating either to the job content itself, the individual, special circumstances surrounding the job or to company policy aimed at attracting and retaining employees.

It could be said that there are four major components in a pay or salary structure. These are:
1. The job rate which relates to the importance of the job, the responsibilities involved in it, and the specific levels of skill and experience required which make mental and physical demands on the job holder.

I

2. Payments associated with encouraging individuals or groups by rewarding them according to their performance. Examples of the methods used are payment by results schemes, share-of-production plans, merit rating or profit-sharing schemes.
3. Special or personal allowances associated with such factors as long service, or scarcity of particular skills or categories of employee. This component also includes recompense for personal or social inconvenience, for example, shift allowances.
4. Fringe benefits such as holidays with pay, pensions, life insurances, cars, etc.

Obviously payment structures differ in the extent to which they incorporate these components, and in the way such components operate and inter-relate. Commonly, however, the first component, the job rate, is used as a basis for calculating performance and other bonuses and for determining the job holder's entitlement to fringe benefits. It is the cornerstone of a sound remuneration system and any errors in job rate relationships will be magnified when total earnings are examined.

Job Evaluation

To ensure a sound remuneration system, it is necessary to develop a pay structure based on the analysis of jobs and on assessment of their relative importance or responsibility.

The technique for doing this is job evaluation, which will provide the data and means for establishing differences between jobs and for developing a job or base rate structure. Without a consistent, acceptable and well thought out base rate structure, few payment systems can remain viable for any length of time. Properly used, job evaluation can provide the means of achieving such a base rate structure. By the development of suitable procedures, job evaluation can additionally provide a means of keeping the base rate structure up to date as jobs alter in scope and content and as new jobs appear.

Much of the job evaluation literature loosely refers to its role in developing fair, logical and equitable pay structures. These are difficult concepts since they appear to relate to abstract standards against which the results of job evaluation should match. It should be stressed that the only standards of fairness and equity which matter are those of the people a job evaluation exercise affects. Thus in so far as this book is concerned we would concur with the comments of the National Board for Prices and Incomes that:

The meanings of 'equity' and 'logic', however, inevitably tend to vary according to the standpoint of different people. The standpoint of management, for instance, need not necessarily be the same as the standpoint of employees. For our part, we would in this context relate 'logic' to the replacement of arbitrary and confused pay differentials by differentials based on common criteria after examination of job contents and conditions. Similarly, we would express the concept of 'equity' as equal pay for work of equal worth, as measured by the particular job evaluation scheme in use.

Job Evaluation Methods

There are many methods of job evaluation, the five *most commonly used* ones being:

> ranking
> grading
> factor comparison
> points rating
> profiling.

Over the last few years, however, the number of methods available has grown as newer ones have been developed—methods such as analytical grading and time span of discretion. Although some methods differ significantly from others, there are, within each, elements common to all. These are discussed in detail in Chapter II but, broadly speaking, the most commonly used methods involve four major stages of work:

1. Analysing and specifying in a written job description the content of a job in terms of responsibilities, knowledge and skills required.
2. Systematically and consistently assessing the job factors involved in each job relative to the demands of other jobs.
3. Producing a rank order of jobs based on the assessments carried out in 2 above, and devising a grade structure so that jobs of similar levels of demand are placed in the same grade.
4. Determining how much money is to be paid for jobs in each grade.

Scope of Job Evaluation

Job evaluation can be used to develop not only pay structures for hourly paid and weekly paid clerical employees, but also salary structures for managers, executives, technicians and other professional employees. Practice varies widely as to the levels at which job evaluation is applied. The Prices and Incomes Board, in a national survey of job evaluation practice carried out in 1967, published the coverage of job evaluation by broad occupational groups. The highest coverage appeared in the managerial category with 30% coverage, followed by staff and non-craft manual employees with 27% and 26% coverage respectively. 11% of craftsmen were covered. One significant feature of these figures is that job evaluation had been used for all types of work. The same survey showed that, although the majority of job evaluation schemes introduced since the war were introduced by large organisations employing over five thousand employees, there was a significant trend towards its use by much smaller organisations. It can be said that organisations of all sizes are finding the technique of increasing value, and the greatest growth rate in the use of the technique is coming from the small to medium sized organisations.

Symptoms of Need for Job Evaluation

Some problems which are frequently encountered in practice, and lead organisations to look afresh at their wage and salary structure are:

1. The pay or salary for jobs of similar responsibility varies widely and this is felt to be unfair by employees.
2. Technical change has brought about changes in job content so that previously difficult jobs are now simple, or simple jobs have become more complex.
3. Previously well defined relationships have been disturbed by changes in the bargaining power of sectional groups.
4. *Ad hoc* reactions by managers to production, market or other pressures have resulted in pay decisions being taken for reasons of expediency, and have upset other parts of the pay structure.
5. There has been drift in payment by results systems, so that total pay for a group has become out of line with that for other groups.
6. The gradual drift of a merit pay scheme into what in practice is a long-service or good time-keeping scheme.
7. Too many different rates have led to inflexibility in the use of labour and high administrative costs or, conversely, too few rates have led to a feeling of unfairness due to lack of differentials.
8. Difficulties have been encountered in recruitment either because potential recruits feel the rate for the job is wrong or too complex in make-up, or they are unwilling to work in

4

a situation where management/employee relationships are poor due to constant bickering about pay.

In many organisations these problems result in employees feeling that the total remuneration system is unfair, inequitable and arbitrary, and even in situations where management itself has been unable to give any logical reasons for the pay differentials that exist. It is not so much the fact that the anomalies exist that matters, but rather the stress, tension and conflict to which they are liable to give rise, and the consequent deterioration in management/employee relationships. At best, management are faced with a continuing trickle of pay claims based on relativities. At worst, management find that due to its imbalance and instability they are in danger of losing control over their payment system.

On the other hand, there are those problems and difficulties caused b remuneration systems which are inappropriate to new or changing situations. For instance, some organisations have found that, whereas in the past pay structures with twenty or thirty grades have not given rise to any major problems, this is no longer true. Pressures for increased productivity and more effective labour utilisation have created requirements for increased flexibility which a twenty- or thirty-grade structure positively impedes. Other organisations have decided on a radical change in the make-up of their payment system following either the abandonment of an incentive or payment-by-results scheme as a result of changes in their production technology, or the replacing of a highly drift-prone payment-by-results scheme with a more controlled one.

For most organisations, there are two basic starting points for considering whether job evaluation can be of value:

1. Dissatisfaction with an existing remuneration system.
2. The realisation that the conditions in which an existing remuneration system operates are likely to alter so radically in the near future that it will cease to have any validity in the new situation.

Other organisations beginning operation in a 'green field' site may take as their starting point the desire to start with a systematic and acceptable remuneration system which, because it is regarded as fair and equitable by its employees, will retain its viability as the scale of operation grows.

The Value of Using Job Evaluation
The importance of using job evaluation lies in its logical, factual and systematic approach to the determination of job relationships.

B
5

Firstly, it is based on facts. Written job descriptions enable discussion to be based on what actually happens in a job, not what people *think* happens, nor what the job was some five or six years ago. Secondly, jobs are compared using common, previously defined criteria so as to increase the objectivity and consistency of the evaluation. Thirdly, the whole process is one of systematically relating jobs one to another by examination of the importance or difficulty of a job. But it cannot be over-stressed that this is by no means a purely technical process, it is also one of policy. The aim is to establish an acceptable rank order of jobs. This means acceptable to management, employees and unions. To management because they have to pay the resulting wage or salary bill; to employees and unions, because they should regard the resultant rank order as fair and equitable. What is fair and equitable is often coloured by traditional relationships: therefore the greater the deviation of a job evaluated rank order of jobs from the norms and expectations of those affected, the greater the dangers of its being unacceptable. But if newly defined job relationships and monetary differentials are accepted as 'right' for the jobs as they are performed at a particular point in time, and if an agreement to this effect is formally made, then, as long as job contents remain the same, management and unions are in a better and more informed position to deal with subsequent claims.

Once a job evaluated structure has been introduced, it provides a disciplined framework for managerial pay decisions. *Ad hoc* reactions to pressures cannot be solved by the simple expedient of a pay increase for a small group of employees which, whilst solving the immediate problem, may result in larger problems later. Management, unless they are to give up the whole job evaluation approach, are forced to relate all pay problems to the total pay structure. Thus the potential impact of individual pay decisions on the pay structure as a whole can be assessed.

The Stages of Introducing Job Evaluation
Very briefly, since these points will be dealt with in later chapters in some detail, the stages of introducing job evaluation are as follows:

Phase I: preparatory
    (a) preparatory work concerned with policy, programme, planning and communications;
    (b) selection of the job evaluation method most appropriate

to the circumstances of an organisation and tailoring it to fit the requirements of that organisation;

(c) establishment of the necessary procedures and training of those applying the scheme.

Phase II: analysis and assessment

(a) communication to the employees concerned what the objectives of the job evaluation exercise are and how the exercise will be carried out;

(b) description, analysis, and evaluation of jobs to define job relationships.

Phase III: building and pricing the structure

(a) positioning of jobs into a number of grades;

(b) financial evaluation of grades.

Phase IV: negotiation, implementation and control

(a) where applicable, negotiation of the new pay structure;

(b) implementation of the new pay structure, perhaps on a phased basis;

(c) establishment of procedures to evaluate new and revised jobs and for maintenance of the system.

Dependent on the job evaluation method used, some of these stages may overlap each other or even vary slightly in their sequence and content.

Other Benefits of Job Evaluation

Job evaluation is not only a valuable tool in reforming pay structures —many other advantages can accrue from its use. Not least of these should be the improvement of management/employee relationships. In our experience the process of applying job evaluation can be used as an opportunity to strengthen management/employee relations and develop increasing understanding of each side's aspirations and viewpoints.

The data resulting from a job evaluation exercise can, however, be valuable in other areas. Job descriptions can be used for:

1. Recruitment, promotion and training purposes as well as providing basic data for manpower planning and management development activities.

2. Informing management about actual rather than theoretical work and organisational situations thus highlighting organisation structure problems, or providing a basis for work simplification and elimination of duplicated functions.

3. Providing useful data for work study and O & M depart-

ments on various aspects such as the under-utilisation of high skills on certain jobs.

In addition, once a job evaluated grade structure has been developed, it can provide the base for the development of more sophisticated cost and budgetary control systems than were previously possible.

Other more indirect by-products have been claimed as a result of the introduction of job evaluation and as an additional justification for its use:

> reduction of lost time as a result of wage disputes;
>
> reduction in the number of individual complaints regarding wages;
>
> reduction in the number of wage and salary anomalies;
>
> reduced labour turnover;
>
> improved morale.

The first three of these would be anticipated as a result of a successful job evaluation exercise. It would, however, be unwise to attribute a direct cause and effect relationship between job evaluation and the remaining two. They will result from the interplay of many influences of which job evaluation might be one.

Conclusion

Before going on, in the next chapter, to describe the various job evaluation techniques, it is perhaps useful to summarise the essential characteristics of job evaluation. These are:

1. Job evaluation is concerned solely with assessing the job—not the man. It is concerned with the work individuals are required to do—it is not a method of assessing efficiency, level of effort, personal performance, or merit of any individual.

2. Job evaluation is not a technique of exact measurement; nor is it, as some have claimed, 'scientific': there is no method of job evaluation which has the exactitude of a mathematical technique. It is a process of assessment based on a series of judgments which contains, therefore, an essential element of subjectivity.

3. Job evaluation is based on facts—on an examination of what employees actually do as opposed to what it is thought they do.

4. It is systematic, since there is a defined sequence of description,

analysis and assessment to be followed for every job evaluated. It is more consistent than rule of thumb methods of pay determination since all jobs under review are matched against uniform criteria.

5. Job evaluation aims to establish acceptable internal pay relationships between jobs within an organisation.

It may perhaps be apt to end this general introduction to the subject by quoting from paragraph 50 of the N.B.P.I's Report on job evaluation:

> The use of job evaluation by an organisation may be taken as an expression of a wider management attitude: that decisions should be based on facts obtained by analysis, that all aspects of an organisation's functioning—systems of payment as well as production and marketing—require conscious planning and control, and that reactions to random pressures should be replaced by systematic attempts to tackle underlying causes.

Chapter II

DIFFERENT METHODS OF JOB ASSESSMENT

The purpose of this chapter is to outline the various job evaluation methods at present commonly being used in industry and commerce. Some have been in operation for many years, whilst others are the result of more recent research, whose advocates claim that they give a greater degree of objectivity and are more relevant to the circumstances of a particular organisation or level of employee, than a more general scheme. However, the fundamental principle remains that, regardless of the system used, the objective of *any* job evaluation exercise is to establish an acceptable rank order of jobs in the particular area under review.

The methods of job evaluation currently in use today tend to fall into one of two main groupings and are referred to as either non-analytical or analytical methods of job evaluation. The difference between them is that basically the non-analytical methods, whilst establishing a grading hierarchy, are non-quantitative, whereas analytical methods are quantitative and the differentials and job values are usually finally expressed in some numerical form.

In this chapter we shall be examining the following methods of job evaluation:

A. *Non-Analytical*	B. *Analytical*
job ranking	points assessment
job classification	factor comparison
	profile method

In addition, we shall mention briefly some other special applications of analytical methods.

A. NON-ANALYTICAL METHODS

Job Ranking

This system of job evaluation is commonly regarded and written about as the simplest method of job evaluation. The principle of job ranking is indeed simple and straightforward, but to apply the method in practice calls for a high degree of personal knowledge on the part of the evaluator of the jobs under review.

The objective of this method is to assess the importance of each job *as a whole* in relation to all of the other jobs being evaluated at the same time. Jobs are not broken down into any component parts or separate factors in order to assess them. The ranking is usually carried out be a committee. The assessors work from their overall knowledge of each job, ideally supplemented by a written description of the duties and responsibilities involved and of the requirements necessary for an individual to be able to undertake the work at an acceptable level. These are known as job descriptions, which are discussed in Appendix I. The assessors simply compare each job against the other jobs, deciding whether it is:

(a) as demanding

(b) more demanding

(c) less demanding

A simple but effective aid to this work is for the assessors to have a set of cards prepared, each having one of the job titles written on it. Having completed cards for all of the jobs in question, comparison is made easier by sorting the cards into order with the most important job at one end and the least important job at the other.

As a result of this exercise, they will, as a first step, be able to prepare a ranking table which is really a list of the jobs in order of importance. In a small organisation or in a particular functional area, all jobs can be listed together, but where jobs under review are more diffuse it is better to prepare separate listings under departmental or other convenient headings, as shown in figure 1.

Production Dept.	Engineering Dept.	Warehouse Dept.
General Supervisor	Supervisor	Supervisor
Supervisor, Production	Leading Hand	Leading Hand
Supervisor, Inspection	Toolmaker	Store-keeper
Leading Hand, Production	Fitter	Receiver
	Electrician	Despatcher
Leading Hand, Inspection	Carpenter	Packer
Inspector	Painter	Stenciller
Machine Operative	Driver	Warehouse Beginner
Handler	Gardener	
	Labourer	

Figure 1. *Drawing up a ranking schedule—the first step*

Having compared jobs 'vertically' the assessors will then, if more than one distinct area is under review, look at the situation 'horizontally' in order to equate jobs of equal worth across the whole area. It is in this phase that the written description of the responsibilities and the requirements necessary to fulfil them is

XYZ ORGANISATION

Job Ranking Schedule

Date...

Production Dept.	Warehouse Dept.	Engineering and Maintenance Dept.	Grade
General Supervisor			8
Supervisor, Production Supervisor, Inspection	Supervisor	Supervisor	7
Leading Hands		Leading Hand	6
	Leading Hand	Toolmaker	5
Inspector		Fitter Painter Electrician Carpenter	4
Machine Operative	Store-Keeper Receiver Despatcher	Driver	3
	Packer Stenciller	Gardener	2
Handler	Warehouse Beginner	Labourer	1

Figure 2. *Job ranking—the grading schedule*

particularly useful, in order to supplement the personal knowledge of the assessors and for them to use when discussing rankings with line management. After this has been done, it is possible to draw up a complete ranking schedule which will show the relative position of all jobs. Jobs of the same ranking are allocated the same grade and a grading structure emerges (see figure 2). The final phase is the attachment of monetary values to the various grade levels.

A more refined method of ranking is achieved by using paired comparisons. Here every job is compared with every other job on the American tournament principle. If a job is considered to be more demanding than the one it is compared with, it scores 3 points, and 1 point is allocated to the job with less demand. If the same demand is present in each job, then each gets 2 points. The scores are added up and a rank order obtained as shown in figure 3.

Job	A	B	C	D	Score Value
A	X	1	2	3	6
B	3	X	3	2	8
C	2	1	X	1	4
D	1	2	3	X	6

Thus the rank order is: 1. B
2. { A
     D
4.   C

Figure 3. *Paired comparisons*

Ranking methods can be used for any level or range of work, but since the results are subjective it is difficult to express the reasons for the resultant positions of some jobs within grades. It is not unusual to use a ranking method when there are a considerable number of jobs to be assessed, although the paired comparison method offers a slight refinement over the straight ranking one. Although it is simple and inexpensive administratively to apply ranking methods in a reasonably stable situation, the results are difficult to maintain and control because the method is dependent upon the evaluators' detailed personal knowledge of the jobs.

To help overcome this it is essential to prepare job descriptions for the jobs under review, even though this takes up a not inconsiderable amount of time. Where ranking is jointly carried out by management and those whose jobs are being evaluated, feelings and values about jobs are inbuilt into the system. This generally makes for a high level of acceptability of the results, and providing there are few jobs and the organisation is in a reasonably stable situation with regard to changes in job content, the system can be used safely. It is a useful technique to use in checking relationships of key jobs within functional groupings and to use as a supplement or cross check with other systems. Some organisations include a ranking exercise as an integral part of their job evaluation system, which may in fact be based on an analytical method.

JOB CLASSIFICATION

As in job ranking, the classification or grading method of job evaluation does not call for a detailed or quantitative analysis of individual parts of the job but is based on the job as a whole. It differs from the job ranking method, however, in that before any

Level or grade	Definition
1.	Very simple tasks of largely physical nature.
2.	Simple tasks carried out in accordance with a small number of clearly defined rules, and which can be carried out after a short period of training of up to 2-3 weeks. The work is checked and closely supervised.
3.	Straight-forward tasks, but involving more complicated routines and requiring a degree of individual knowledge and alertness, as the work is subject to occasional check.
4.	Tasks calling for the independent arrangement of work, the exercise of some initiative, where little supervision is needed. Detailed familiarity with one or more branches of established procedure required.
5.	Routine work, but involving an individual degree of responsibility for answering non-routine queries and/or exercising some measure of control over a small group of staff.
6.	Non-routine work, involving co-ordination of several lower grade functions, possibly some measure of control over small group of staff. Also non-routine work involving recognised individual knowledge and some responsibility without follow-up.
7.	Work necessitating responsibility for sections involved on routine tasks and/or where there are also individual tasks to be undertaken, calling for specialist knowledge.

Figure 4. *Job classification schedule*

evaluation of jobs takes place the number of grading levels (i.e. those levels where it is felt there should be a monetary differential) and the criteria for determining the type of work and responsibility to meet these levels are defined. Before the review begins, a schedule along the lines shown in figure 4 should have been prepared.

It is usual in job classification to select one or two jobs from each of the levels in the grading structure and prepare descriptions of the duties, responsibilities, and requirements necessary to fulfil them to an acceptable level of performance. These jobs are known as *benchmark* or *key* jobs, and indicate to the assessors, management and employees, the type of work and level of responsibility at each grade in the structure. They must, therefore, be readily identifiable and it must be accepted by all concerned that the selected jobs at each level are worth a higher rate of pay than those in the grade below. When using a classification or grading method, monetary values can be attached either at the beginning or at the end of the actual evaluation exercise. Having selected the benchmark or key jobs, the other jobs in the area under review are compared against them and the descriptive criteria, and the appropriate match is made. This will then indicate the grade.

The classification approach can be used to evaluate jobs on an organisation-wide basis which fall into like groups and/or families, such as secretaries and technicians. Examples of this approach are shown in Appendix II.

The Institute of Office Management (I.O.M.) has published a grading scheme which provides criteria to define distinct levels of clerical work between which monetary differentials are justified and into which any clerical job can be placed. Their full classification schedule gives examples of individual tasks and complete jobs under both grade and functional headings (e.g. payroll, cash control, sales enquiries, orders and invoicing). The definitions and examples advocated by the I.O.M. are shown in Appendix III.

Grading or classification systems can be applied to all types of work but the method is itself a rather blunt measuring instrument in that it attempts to fit all jobs into a series of broadly defined levels. In practice jobs are frequently found to have certain features fitting more than one level and thus the final classification tends to be subjective and inconsistent. Like ranking methods, these systems often lack sufficient detailed analysis and specification to enable management to pick up changes in job content quickly and accurately. Consequently it is difficult to maintain an adequate

15

control of the resultant wage and salary structure. Classification methods may be relatively cheap to apply, but unless they are applied to limited ranges of like work such as the I.O.M. clerical grading, or to a single function such as industrial engineering, or within a small organisation with a clear cut narrow range of work, the results are likely to be less than satisfactory.

Advantages and Disadvantages of Non-Analytical Methods
The main advantage of non-analytical methods is that results can be obtained more quickly and cheaply than by analytical methods.

The main disadvantage of non-analytical methods is that they do not quantify differences between jobs and therefore the true significance of job changes cannot, at times, be adequately assessed. Non-analytical methods tend to be the ones incurring the greatest subjectivity where, particularly in job ranking, the individual could be assessed rather than the job. As quantitative differentials are not achieved by using non-analytical methods, difficulty is sometimes experienced in deciding where to draw the line that defines a grading difference. This leads to a disadvatage in that there can be difficulty in communicating to employees *precisely why* a job is in a particular grade or why a job should not be up-graded because of additions to it. Because of the difficulties previously mentioned, there is a danger of up-grading jobs for comparatively minor additions to them. This results in a leap-frogging activity which is dangerous and which, if not checked, will soon result in the grading structure becoming unbalanced.

B. *ANALYTICAL METHODS*

In this section we shall deal with points assessment, factor comparison, and the profile method. Analytical grading, Hay/MSL, time span, and the direct consensus methods are described in appendices.

POINTS ASSESSMENT
The points method of job evaluation is at present the most common of the job evaluation systems in use. Unlike the ranking and classification methods, each job is considered under a number of specific aspects or factors and given an appropriate number of points related to a pre-defined scale. The same factors are used for every job, and the total points score for each job places it in its appropriate position in the rank order, e.g. a job with 150 points ranks higher than a job with 140 points.

The same points assessment plan is not normally used to cover the entire range of jobs in an organisation but common practice is to have separate plans for, say, manual, clerical and managerial jobs. The reason for this is that the differing nature of the work calls for assessment by different factors and for giving different emphasis to them. For example, physical requirements and working conditions are significant at manual levels but insignificant for managerial jobs.

Points assessment schemes may be broadly divided into two types:

1. Either widely used existing systems where the characteristics, weighting and points values are pre-determined, or schemes which are adaptations of these.

2. Schemes which are tailor made to suit the particular circumstances of the application. In these schemes it is usual to select a number of job characteristics and assign to them a range of points and weighting. A number of benchmark jobs are assessed and the points range and weighting originally assigned is tested for its appropriateness.

An illustration of a points assessment scheme that is widely used in industry is shown in Appendix IV.

The stages in introducing a points assessment scheme are as follows:

determine the job factors or characteristics to be used;

determine points ranges for each factor, with or without weighting;

divide the factors into levels or degrees;

select a representative number of benchmark jobs;

analyse each benchmark job under each of the factor headings and assign a points score from within the predetermined points range;

determine weighting, if this has not been done previously;

review the initial results of the evaluations of the benchmark jobs to see if the resultant grading hierarchy is relevant to the needs of the organisation;

assuming that the test results are satisfactory, evaluate the remainder of the jobs, placing them in a rank order according to the points scored;

determine where the grade lines will be drawn;

assign a financial value to each grade.

These stages are discussed in more detail below.

1. *Determine the job factors to be used in the plan*
   The number of factors used in points assessment vary from plan to plan, but the essential aspects to bear in mind when undertaking this work are:

(a) the factors used must bear relevance to the jobs being assessed (e.g. it is of no value to include responsibilities for the work of others if the jobs are basically clerical, manual or craft orientated and do not call for any supervisory responsibilities on the part of the job-holders);

(b) care must be taken to ensure that no factor is duplicated; where there is any risk that a single aspect of a job can be assessed twice under different headings, definitions must be clear and precise (e.g. there may well be an overlap between 'training time' and 'experience' if these are used as separate factors);

(c) employment conditions such as shift work, night work, necessary overtime, are not a part of job evaluation. These and similar features should not be used as factors in any job evaluation exercise, but should be compensated for separately.

Some plans utilize many factors, but there is a tendency now for the number to be reduced as new job evaluation plans are introduced or existing ones revised.

All factors used normally relate to the following broad characteristics of work:

> skills required
> mental requirements
> physical requirements
> responsibilities
> working conditions;

and several plans use these as main factors. Other points assessment plans subdivide these, or similar main factors, into sub-factors; other plans may have a larger number of main factors.

Having regard to the points referred to above, it is stressed that the selection of factors, and possibly sub-factors, is essentially a matter for the organisation concerned. The nature of the jobs to be assessed and the general working environment will significantly influence the decisions to be made.

It is possible to list many job characteristics that can be used in a scheme either as main factors or as sub-factors. Examples of headings used for hourly paid employees are shown in Appendices IV and V and for clerical employees in Appendix VI. When determining the factors best suited for the jobs to be evaluated, it should be borne in mind that the selection of too many factors in points assessment systems can be unnecessarily time-consuming, and increases the danger of assigning points more than once to the same aspect of the job. Nonetheless, it is necessary to use sub-factors of the main factors in order to maintain consistency, since assessors will find it difficult to account for all aspects of the main factors in the same manner.

Having selected the factors to be used, it is essential, for successful operation that they are defined in writing, so that all concerned know exactly what criteria are being used when the analysis and assessment of the job takes place. Having established the main definition for the factor, it is necessary to break the factor down into various levels or degrees of importance, which in turn must be defined. To illustrate how these definitions can be expressed, an example of a factor, together with degree definitions, is shown in figure 5.

Factor: Responsibility for the Work of Others

This factor appraises the continuous responsibility of the employee for the satisfactory work performance of other employees in the organisation.

1st Degree	No responsibility for the work of others.
2nd Degree	Part-time guidance of the work of others. Assigns duties, gives instruction, checks work and handles ordinary difficulties. However, employee spends a large part of his time doing work similar to that done by other members of the group.
3rd Degree	Employee spends majority of his time guiding the work of others. Assigns duties, gives frequent instruction, checks work and handles ordinary difficulties. May spend part of his time doing work similar to that done by members of the group.
4th Degree	Responsible for maintaining satisfactory work performance without maintaining a close check over specific work details. Advises and directs during the installation stage of new techniques, practices and procedures.
5th Degree	Responsible for maintaining satisfactory work performance of more than one organisational level of employee. Subordinate employees assume responsibility for certain aspects of work planning, standards and output in the unit.

Degree	1	2	3	4	5
Points	0	11	19	32	55

Figure 5. *Breaking down a factor into degrees or levels*

2. *Determine points ranges for each factor, with or without weighting*
It is extremely unlikely that the factors chosen will be of equal importance and because of this the factors are weighted. Weighting simply means giving a greater value to some factors than to others. There are a number of ways of doing this:

(a) a greater number of points may be allocated to some of the factors, or

(b) the same number of points may be allocated to each factor, but a multiplier is afterwards applied, so that the difference in values of the factor are reflected in the points scale.

There is a great variation in the weightings chosen in practice—each organisation must ensure that the weightings used produce a sensible and acceptable ranking of jobs. It is therefore essential to test out possible alternatives before coming to a conclusion. There are a number of commonly used predetermined systems (e.g. The National Electrical Manufacturers Association) which can be used, but which require validating prior to introduction in an organisation.

3. *Assessment of jobs*
In the majority of cases where points assessment schemes are in operation the assessment of jobs is carried out by an assessment panel or committee. One of the first tasks of the committee is to select a number of key jobs and undertake a trial run to test the validity of the choice of factors and weightings. These key jobs are readily identifiable, and they should number at least twenty. Apart from being readily identifiable they should be drawn on a representative basis from as wide a range of jobs as possible covering varying degrees of skill and working conditions.

Job descriptions for these selected key jobs should be prepared. Having observed all of the key jobs in operation, the committee will assess for each job the points score under each factor heading. It is useful at this stage to prepare factor sheets for each of the factors used in the plan and included and agreed for all of the key jobs. The various factor scores for each job when added together give a total score for each job. In some schemes a constant number of points is added to the variable points which have been allocated by the assessors. This is called a *datum*, which is usually 100 points.

20

The point values of jobs scoring 60, 71 and 80 therefore become 160, 171 and 180. The reasons for adding the datum are that some organisations feel that all jobs have a minimum level of demand which should be recognised, and that the datum itself tends to stabilise any likely inaccuracies which have crept in due to human judgment in allocating precise points.

At the end of this exercise, a schedule of the key jobs, together with the evaluated number of points can be prepared and scrutinised for any apparent inconsistencies. If these evaluations appear logical, further progress can be made with the rest of the programme, using the established points values for the key jobs under each factor as guide posts when undertaking the further assessments. If not acceptable, revision of the factors and their weightings should be undertaken until a satisfactory result is achieved.

4. *Drawing grade lines and financial evaluations*
The next point to consider is how many grades it is practical to have in the scheme. This may be done by breaking the total points available down to a number of grades, using an arithmetical or geometrical progression. Figure 6 illustrates this.

Range of Points Scored Arithmetic 300 (minimum base points allowance)	Grade	Geometric
350	1	300–330
351–400	2	331–365
401–450	3	366–405
451–500	4	406–445
501–550	5	446–490
551–600	6	491–540
601–650	7	541–595
651–700	8	596–655
701–750	9	656–725
751–800	10	726–800

Figure 6. *Points conversion schedule*

In some cases the needs of a situation suggest that the grades should not have equal points ranges. This aspect and the determination of the number of grades in a structure are discussed later, in Chapter III.

These then are the basic steps to be followed when undertaking a points evaluation exercise. Although the principles outlined should be followed, it is important to realise that any scheme must be devised to take account of the particular circumstances existing in the areas where jobs are to be reviewed. It is generally dangerous to attempt to use points evaluation schemes which may well have been very successful in other organisations. Appendices V and VI are illustrations of two points evaluation plans in use today which meet the needs of the organisations using them. They are given as examples merely to illustrate the basis on which a points method can be established.

As we have said, points assessment systems broadly fall into two categories, namely the predetermined systems specific to particular ranges of work, and the tailor-made systems devised for particular ranges of work within a single enterprise. Predetermined systems lack flexibility and should be adopted only after a trial run. It may be more expensive in time and cost for an organisation to devise its own scheme but, in the long term, it is likely to be more appropriate and more acceptable to all concerned. The major weakness of all points assessment systems is their numerical rating scale, which tends both to give a spurious sense of accuracy to job assessment and to cause arguments over what are in fact minor job differences of little value. Although the points assessment schemes can be more effectively controlled subsequently than can non-analytical systems, difficulties tend to arise as job changes occur, due to the fact that both the rating scale and the grades are expressed in numerical points. It is hard to argue convincingly that a change in work method does not call for an additional point under some work characteristics. If the additional point altered the job grade it could cause dissatisfaction at best and a chain reaction of demands for up-grading at worst.

FACTOR COMPARISON

In the factor comparison method of job evaluation jobs are examined using a predetermined monetary scale for each factor and the total of the factor values so determined for each job represents its evaluated cash rate. The significance is that, once the factors have been identified, the jobs are evaluated in cash terms rather than using a numerical points scale.

The initial stages are basically the same as for the points assessment method and as a first step job factors are selected. However, in factor comparison schemes there tend to be fewer factors used than for points assessment methods. Sub-factors are not used. For hourly paid personnel the common main factors used are:

skill

mental requirements

physical requirements

responsibility

working conditions

Key jobs are then selected and job descriptions prepared. It is, however, important that the key jobs should be considered to have the right internal relationships to each other and be considered to be paid adequately in relation to the local labour market. It is no use, for example, selecting as a key job one in which the monetary rate is under dispute.

The key jobs are then ranked under each of the factors, as shown in figure 7 (overleaf).

The next step is for the panel of assessors to decide for each job how much of the current rate is paid for each factor. A schedule can be built using the matrix shown in figure 8 (page 25).

Comparisons are then made between the ranking and the agreed factor rate. This serves as a useful cross check on the suitability of the key jobs originally selected, and it is recommended that a ranking/factor rate schedule is drawn up at this stage, as shown in figure 9 (page 26).

The final stage is to prepare a factor comparison schedule, which shows the pence per hour value of all of the key jobs under each of the factor headings. Using this as a matrix, other jobs can be compared against the key jobs under each factor heading and a factor value assessed. The sum total of these factor values represents the cash rate for the job in question. An example of a factor comparison schedule, with key jobs illustrated, is shown in figure 10.

Using the schedule as a guide, other jobs are compared, under each of the factor headings, against the key jobs and a monetary rate calculated. It is then usual to group rates of a like value into job grades, but Chapter III deals in more detail with this aspect.

The factor comparison scheme described above is specific to shop floor levels, but a number of adaptations have been used for managerial levels. The method first devised by Benge has had wider usage in the USA than here, where the system is felt to be somewhat complex to apply and difficult to explain. The use of financial figures for the rating scale tends to colour judgments and the need to determine how much of a current key job rate is being paid for a job characteristic or a factor is highly subjective and suspect. It appears attractive because its rating scale is geared to the existing pay structure. On the other hand it is less flexible than other analytical methods, especially in situations of method or technical change. Like all analytical methods it goes into greater detail and therefore, although more factually based, it is more expensive in time and cost than a non-analytical method.

Rank	Mental Requirements	Physical Requirements	Responsibility	Skill	Working Conditions
1	Instrument Making	Labouring	Die Making	Die Making	Rigging
2	Die Making	Rigging	Instrument Making	Instrument Making	Painting
3	Pattern Making	Carrying	Pattern Making	Pattern Making	Machine Greasing
4	Fitting	Cleaning	Fitting	Turning	Core Moulding
5	Crane Driving	Die Making	Crane Driving	Rigging	Cleaning
6	Turning	Core Moulding	Turning	Fitting	Truck Driving
7	Core Moulding	Truck Driving	Machine Greasing	Crane Driving	Crane Driving
8	Rigging	Machine Greasing	Rigging	Core Moulding	Turning
9	Machine Greasing	Turning	Core Moulding	Painting	Die Making
10	Print Storekeeping	Fitting	Carrying	Print Storekeeping	Carrying
11	Painting	Painting	Truck Driving	Truck Driving	Fitting
12	Carrying	Pattern Making	Painting	Machine Greasing	Labouring
13	Truck Driving	Crane Driving	Print Storekeeping	Carrying	Print Storekeeping
14	Cleaning	Instrument Making	Cleaning	Cleaning	Pattern Making
15	Labouring	Print Storekeeping	Labouring	Labouring	Instrument Making

Figure 7.   *Ranking table*

24

	Current Rate Per Hour	Mental Reqts.		Physical Reqts.		Responsibility		Skill		Working Conds.	
		%	d	%	d	%	d	%	d	%	d
Carrying	76	16	12	34	26	20	15	12	9	18	14
Cleaning	66	9	6	36	24	10	7	9	6	36	23
Core Moulding	101	21	21	21	21	$10\frac{1}{2}$	17	17	17	24	25
Crane Driving	95	24	23	7	7	28	26	20	19	21	20
Die Making	148	18	26	15	22	28	42	28	42	11	16
Fitting	100	23	24	13	12	30	30	21	21	13	13
Instrument Making	113	26	29	4	5	34	38	31	35	5	6
Labouring	66	6	4	64	42	6	6	4	4	18	12
Machine Greasing	96	19	18	19	18	21	20	12	12	29	28
Painting	85	16	14	13	11	14	12	19	16	38	32
Pattern Making	105	24	25	8	8	32	34	28	30	8	8
Print Storekeeping	55	30	16	7	4	18	10	27	15	18	10
Rigging	133	15	20	24	32	14	18	17	23	30	40
Truck Driving	80	12	10	25	20	18	14	17	14	28	22
Turning	102	21	22	16	16	21	22	24	24	18	18

Figure 8. *Percentage of rate per factor*

	Mental Rqts.		Physical Rqts.		Respon- sibility		Skill		Working Conditions	
	Rank	d	Rank	d	Rank	d	Rank	d	Rank	d
Carrying	12	12	3	26	10	15	13	9	10	14
Cleaning	14	6	4	24	14	7	14	7	5	23
Core Moulding	7	21	6	21	9	17	8	17	4	25
Crane Driving	5	23	13	7	5	21	7	19	7	20
Die Making	2	26	5	22	1	42	1	42	9	16
Fitting	4	24	10	13	4	30	6	21	11	13
Instrument Making	1	29	14	5	2	38	2	35	15	6
Labouring	15	4	1	42	15	4	15	4	12	12
Machine Greasing	9	18	8	18	7	20	12	12	3	28
Painting	11	14	11	11	12	12	9	16	2	32
Pattern Making	3	25	12	8	3	34	3	30	14	8
Print Storekeeping	10	16	15	4	13	10	10	15	13	10
Rigging	8	20	2	32	8	18	5	23	1	40
Truck Driving	13	10	7	20	11	14	11	14	6	22
Turning	6	22	9	16	6	22	4	24	8	18

Figure 9. *Ranking/factor rate schedule*

'rly ate nce	Mental Reqts.	Physical Reqts.	Responsibility	Skill	Working Conditions
1					
2					
3					
4	Labouring	Print	Labouring	Labouring	
5		Storekeeping Instrument Making			
6	Cleaning				Instrument Making
7		Crane Driving	Cleaning	Cleaning	
8		Pattern Making			Pattern Making
9				Carrying	
0	Truck Driving		Print Storekeeping		Print Storekeeping
1		Painting			
2	Carrying		Painting	Machine Greasing	Labouring
3		Fitting			Fitting
4	Printing		Truck Driving	Truck Driving	Carrying
5			Carrying	Print Storekeeping	
6	Print Storekeeping	Turning		Printing	Die Making
7			Core Moulding	Core Moulding	
8	Machine Greasing	Machine Greasing	Rigging		Turning
9				Crane Driving	
0	Rigging	Truck Driving	Machine Greasing		Crane Driving
1	Core Moulding	Core Moulding		Fitting	
2	Turning	Die Making	Turning		Truck Driving
3	Crane Driving			Rigging	Cleaning
4	Fitting	Cleaning		Turning	
5	Pattern Making		Crane Driving		Core Moulding
6	Die Making	Carrying			
7					
8					Machine Greasing
9	Instrument Making				
0			Fitting	Pattern Making	
1					
2		Rigging			Printing
3					
4			Pattern Making		
5				Instrument Making	
6					
7					
8			Instrument Making		
9					
0					Rigging
1					
2		Labouring	Die Making	Die Making	

ure 10. *Factor comparison schedule*

27

PROFILE METHOD

Analytical methods of job evaluation generally have three common elements: a set of job factors or characteristics; a rating or assessment scale; and a method of weighting the more important characteristics.

The profile method was devised by Urwick, Orr & Partners Limited in 1960 and has been fairly widely used in a number of different industries and for different levels of employees. It has these common elements, but is in detail tailor-made to suit a specific organisation or industry situation.

In the profile method there is:

1. A comprehensive group of clearly defined job characteristics from which a company can select those which are appropriate both to the range of work and the level of jobs being evaluated, i.e. hourly paid, managerial, etc.

2. A rating scale (which is common in all types of application), that differs from those used in most analytical methods, in that it does not deal in numerical points or money, but rather in levels of job demand where each level reflects a clearly identifiable difference in demand.

3. Weighting of characteristics specific to an organisation and reflecting their technical requirements and social values.

Type of Characteristic Used

The profile method is based on the following premises:

1. The job holder can only bring to his work knowledge and a given range of physical, mental, and social aptitudes or, as they are commonly called, skills: therefore, the job he holds cannot make demands beyond these.

2. The level of the demands required to perform a job is determined by such factors as:
   (a) the nature of the work;
   (b) the way in which management has set up the job;
   (c) the degree of responsibility which management assigns to the job holder;
   (d) the physical environment in which the work is being carried out.

Basically, we are concerned therefore with six main job factors, which are:

(i) responsibility
(ii) knowledge
(iii) work environment
(iv) physical aptitudes
(v) mental aptitudes
(vi) social aptitudes

Each of these main factors is an amalgam of a number of different elements or work characteristics, which make it difficult to assess consistently the total value of a main factor for each job being evaluated. Thus it is necessary to break each of the main factors into its constituent parts during the actual assessment or rating of jobs. A typical breakdown of main factors for hourly paid jobs would be:

(i) *responsibility:* this will cover, as appropriate, such sub-factors as the use of expensive resources, exercise of discretion, keeping of records, accountability for money, etc.;

(ii) *knowledge:* knowledge sub-factors include knowledge of tools, equipment, processes, and procedures;

(iii) *work environment:* this includes sub-factors such as humidity, noise, working in restricted spaces, industrial disease and safety—and, possibly even more important, those which are generally considered to be socially and psychologically disagreeable; for example, it includes working in isolation, or performing short-cycle highly repetitive work, which calls for close mental attention and thus fails to give the job holder any control of his pattern of work or carry relief in normal social contact with his fellow workers;

(iv) *physical:* here we are concerned with such sub-factors as physical stamina, the demand for sensory discrimination, and for co-ordinated movements;

(v) *mental:* sub-factors could include judgment, memory, spatial capacity, concentration, numerical capacity;

(vi) *social:* sub-factors include the need to communicate clearly, to work in a team, or to have contact with others outside the immediate working group.

The main factors and certain sub-characteristics will vary according to the range and level of work being covered. For example, under physical aptitudes and work environment few sub-characteristics ever figure in managerial applications: for managerial evaluation knowledge is divided into the following sub-characteristics:

special knowledge

management knowledge

co-ordinative knowledge

knowledge of company policy, plans and procedures.

The framework of intellectual skills is based on information handling for problem solving and decision making, and covers recognition, memory, exploratory and focused thinking, and evaluation.

Devising a Rating Scale

It is difficult for people to rank consistently more than four to five different items, or equally to recognise minor differences such as those represented in a numerical scale of 1, 2, 3, 4, 5. Thus the rating scale is not set up in terms of numerical or financial points, but rather it consists of four different levels of job demand, each level representing an increasing difference of 50% to 100% more than the preceding one. In making an assessment, raters are therefore asked to place a tick in one of the levels for each sub-factor or characteristic. From the assessor's viewpoint this helps him to concentrate on clearly recognisable differences in job demand: from the standpoint of those whose jobs are being evaluated, higher and lower ratings are then not only felt to be fairer and therefore more acceptable, but are also easily identifiable.

Weighting of Factors or Characteristics

The selection of job factors to be weighted is an important issue, since this determines the ultimate ordering of jobs. If this ultimate ordering runs too widely counter to the views on, and attitudes about, job values in an organisation, the resultant base rate structure will be unacceptable. There is therefore a need to ensure that the weighting used will take these sufficiently into account to achieve a generally acceptable result.

The profile method seeks to do this normally through obtaining the views of a joint management/union group on the appropriate relationships of a number of key or benchmark jobs. The approach is as follows:

1. Selecting a number of benchmark or reference jobs which reflect the total range of work being evaluated.
2. Agreeing an acceptable ordering of these by carrying out a global paired comparison of these jobs as described earlier in this chapter.
3. Quantifying the individual profiles by assigning numerical

values to each of the levels in the rating scale. The same range of scoring is used for each sub-characteristic.

4. The weighting necessary to match the two sets of data (2 and 3 on preceding page) is then calculated.

Thus weighting occurs at the end of the first phase of the application.

It will be seen that the system provides a common basis for tailor-making a system specific to the needs of a particular organisation, through its method of selection of appropriate characteristics, its ease of levels for the assessment scale, and its consensus method of determining weighting. The system lends itself to speed of application since the rating scales avoid unnecessary arguments over the precise allocation of points.

Mechanics of Application of the Profile Method
Broadly the system has three distinct phases in its application:

1. (a) the setting up of a joint central committee consisting of management and union or appropriate employee representatives, to be responsible for evaluating jobs and ensuring consistency of assessment;

   (b) an examination of the range of work being evaluated in order to select appropriate characteristics and benchmark or reference jobs which must be representative of both the range of work and, where unions are involved, the disposition of their membership;

   (c) the preparation of detailed written descriptions of benchmark jobs;

   (d) the assessment, i.e. profiling, of benchmark jobs (figure 11, overleaf, illustrates the benchmark job profiling form);

   (e) the ranking of benchmark jobs and determination of the weighting factor as outlined earlier.

   This work is carried out by the central committee.

2. (a) selection and training of the number of assessment teams necessary to complete profiles for all the jobs to be evaluated—this training includes a detailed study of the benchmark jobs and of the levels of individual characteristics allocated to each of them; thus consistency of assessment is ensured throughout the exercise (the form used by teams to assess jobs is illustrated in figure 12.);

   (b) the setting up of procedures for reviewing completed profiles ensuring their accuracy and consistency.

JOB: Chief Process Controller
DEPARTMENT: Process Control

No. Characteristic	Level of Characteristic			
	Exceptional	High	Moderate	Low
I. Responsibility				
A. In use of resources		✓		
B. Influence on effective use of resources	✓			
C. etc.				
D. etc.				
II. Knowledge				
A. Special	✓			
B. Management practices, processes & techniques			✓	
C. Co-ordinating			✓	
D. Company policies, plans & procedures			✓	
III. Mental Skills				
A. Comprehension—handling information	✓			
B. Memory	✓			
C. Exploratory or creative thinking			✓	
D. Deductive or focussed thinking		✓		
E. Evaluation		✓		
IV. Social Skills				
A. Communication—oral		✓		
B. Communication—written		✓		
C. Working with and through other people		✓		
D. Maintaining external contacts				✓
(etc.) • • •	• • •	• • •	• • •	• • •

Date:

Profiled:

Profiled by:

Date Checked:

Figure 11. *Illustration of part of completed profile of a benchmark job in an executive job evaluation*

DEPARTMENT: W. Division

Levels of Characteristics

Characteristic	exceptional	4	high	3	moderate	2	low	1
II. *Knowledge* A. Special	Construction Mgr. XYZ Division Commercial Mgr. LMN Division Chief Design Engineer	✓	District Mgr. LMN Division Chief Commercial Administrator Divisional Accountant		Senior Estimator Assistant Div. Personnel Adviser Purchasing Officer Grade II		Accounts Mgr. XYZ Division Asst. Site Engineer OPQ Division	
B. Management Practices Processes and Techniques	Group Financial Director Construction Mgr. XYZ Division Asst. General Mgr.		Group Personnel Manager Commercial Mgr. LMN Division Site Engineer	✓	Commercial Administrator Senior Estimator Wage & Salary Officer		Purchasing Officer Grade II Accounts Officer Senior Estimator Grade II	
C. Co-ordinating	Group Financial Director Commercial Mgr. LMN Division Group Personnel Director	✓	District Mgr. LMN Division District Engineer XYZ Division Divisional Accountant		Commercial Administrator Senior Site Engineer Group Welfare Officer		Wage & Salary Officer Asst. Site Engineer OPQ Division Senior Estimator	
(etc.)								

Profiled by:

Date Passed by Central Reviewing Committee.................

Figure 12. *Illustration of part of a job profile form for a non-benchmark job used in an executive job evaluation*

33

3.   (a) the classification of jobs into like activities and the rank ordering of jobs under each of these activities;
      (b) checking of obviously out-of-line jobs within each activity and across the activities;
      (c) the building up of an appropriate grade structure according to common job features and job scores;
      (d) devising payment levels for each grade.

The last two tasks are usually given to a separate management committee.

Profiling, like the better types of points assessment methods, can be applied to all levels of work although the job factors chosen naturally differ as between manual, management, etc. The method incorporates in its rating scale, with its concept of significant differences, what is known from research of the human capacity to discriminate differences in physical objects, and thus is capable of greater consistency in application. In its method of weighting characteristics it also ensures that the organisation's values are built into the resulting wage structure. Its maintenance and subsequent control is facilitated by its rating scale in that demands for up-grading cannot be based on minor changes in job content, nor on single point differences. The time and cost of application in smaller organisations is similar to that of other analytical methods, but in a larger organisation it is cheaper and more quickly applied without loss of consistency of assessment.

OTHER SPECIAL METHODS

There are a number of other job evaluation methods which have been developed by consultants or by private organisations. The most widely used of these in this country are described in the appendices at the back of this book.

The first method to mention is the *direct consensus method*, basically using the paired comparison approach and involving all interested parties in its application. It is described in more detail in Appendix VII.

Appendix VIII describes the *analytical grading system* developed by the British Broadcasting Corporation some years ago. It evaluates all the posts within the organisation under five factors.

Another method developed by a consultant firm is the *Hay/MSL* executive job evaluation system which is briefly described in Appendix IX. This method is also basically an analytical one.

In Appendix X the *time span of discretion* method of evaluating jobs is described. This was first developed by Professor Elliott

Jaques at the Glacier Metal Company some years ago. It is a single factor system and applicable for evaluating all levels of work. More recently Dr. T. T. Paterson has developed a *decision band method* which sets up a job evaluation hierarchy based on the level of decision making.

Readers who wish to have more details of the methods of job evaluation discussed in this book will find a reading list at the back.

CHAPTER III

USING THE RESULTS OF JOB EVALUATION TO BUILD THE BASIC RATE STRUCTURE

In the previous chapter a number of methods of analysing work and assessing relative job content were described, so that jobs can be placed in some kind of order relationship according to their different demands for knowledge, skill, etc. The next problem is how to use this information to build up a *basic rate structure* which adequately reflects the rank order of jobs as established by job evaluation. In this chapter we are concerned with trying to determine how much money has to be paid for different occupations with varying levels of job demands.

Unfortunately, there are no scientific principles to guide us in this process. The question of how much money should be paid cannot be deduced in a completely objective fashion. Such problems as labour shortage, union pressure, market rates, company profitability and employee attitudes all affect the answer in varying proportions from time to time. In general, however, management can approach the problem by looking at its existing payment rates, comparing these with rates paid in other organisations, and then deciding how much they can afford and need to pay for different occupations in order to build up an acceptable and competitive basic rate structure.

Methods of Relating Job Assessments to Rates of Pay
The content and sequence of work involved in translating job assessment results into money varies as between different job evaluation methods. For convenience, the steps in each of the five methods already described in Chapter II are summarised in figure 13. From this figure the following variations can be seen:
1.   Ranking, points assessment and profiling have three separate steps in the process of determining job rates of pay:
     (a)   the assessment of jobs in terms of relative job demand;
     (b)   the grouping of jobs with like levels of work demands into a number of job grades;

36

(c) the assigning of money to each job grade.

The difference between the three systems is in the method of assessing jobs. Ranking is non-quantitative, whereas, in points assessment and profiling, job assessments can be quantified.

2. In the classification method there are also three separate steps but in different sequence:
    (a) the number of job grades to be used is selected first;
    (b) jobs are assessed by placing them in the appropriate grade;
    (c) monetary values are assigned to each job grade.

In some cases the monetary values are determined before jobs are allocated to their appropriate grades.

3. Factor comparison is a two-step process:
    (a) the rate for the job is determined during assessment through the use of a monetary scale;
    (b) a number of job grades are identified on the basis of like levels of payment.

Most methods separate the processes of job assessment, job grading and financial evaluation, and indeed carry them out in this order. In our experience this approach enables a higher level of objectivity to be attained at each stage and tends therefore to result in a payment structure which is more easily accepted and better defended in its subsequent negotiation, implementation and maintenance.

BUILDING THE BASIC RATE STRUCTURE
ANALYSIS OF PRESENT SITUATION

Before trying to establish new basic rates, as we mentioned earlier, it is necessary to get a bird's eye view of how far present basic rate payments in the organisation match the job relationships established by job evaluation. To do this it is necessary first to identify all payments that are associated with the job factors included in the job evaluation system which has been used. For example, an analysis of many pay systems will show that special payments for working under poor conditions or at heights are often made. Or again, an organisation may have used special allowances to attract a certain grade of employee in short supply. At this stage all these special payments should be added to calculate the basic rate for each job. Once this has been done, the easiest way in which to get an overall picture of the present structure as it relates to the job evaluation results is to draw a scattergram in which existing basic rates are plotted as against job evaluation scores. A line or a curve of best fit can be drawn showing the general level of basic rate payments as illustrated in figure 14.

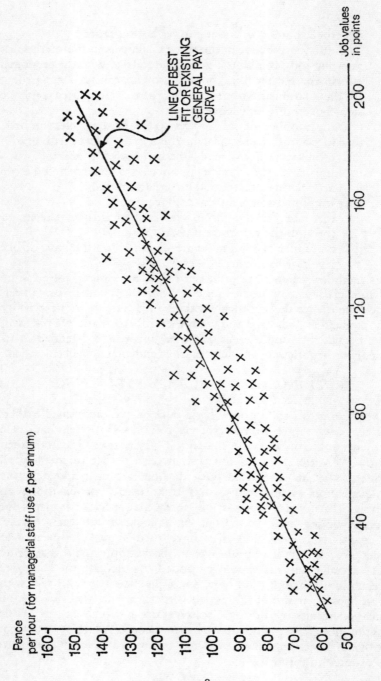

Pence per hour (for managerial staff use £ per annum)

LINE OF BEST FIT OR EXISTING GENERAL PAY CURVE

Job values in points

Figure 14. *Scattergram to establish present basic rates of payment*

38

In this illustration, the organisation's basic rates range from 5/–
to a little over 12/– per hour. In this case the best fit for the general
level is a straight line : some organisations' payment rates would
tend to form a curve rather than a straight line.

GRADING OF JOBS

Scrutinising the Results of the Job Evaluation
As already pointed out, we start the process of grading with a rank
order of jobs which have to be grouped together into a number of
grades. Before any decisions can be made on the number of grades
required or on where grade lines can be drawn, this list should be
carefully scrutinised to identify any jobs which appear to be wrongly
placed relative to other jobs or to other job relationships. Such jobs
are said to be 'out of line'. Jobs can be out of line in terms of their
ranking relationship with other jobs in their own function or like
activity, e.g. within a group of different inspection jobs: alternatively
they can be out of line with other jobs of similar value but in
different functions or activities. It is, therefore, helpful before
carrying out a detailed scrutiny of the overall results to classify
the total range of jobs being evaluated into their functional groups.
The table below illustrates this.

Plant Management	Engineering Services—Maintenance & Tool Room
Marketing & Selling	Inspection
Finance & Costing	Transport
Industrial Engineering	Materials Handling & Stores
Technical Services & Engineering	Machine Shops
Personnel & Training	Assembly
Research & Development	Ancillary Services

The type of industry and the size of the organisation affect the
choice and degree of breakdown: for example, in a large construction organisation quantity surveying might be a separate
activity: or again in the chemical industry there would be a category
of 'process workers'. Once the classification has been made, jobs
should be placed in descending order of value under each heading.
It is useful to post these results on a board, so that jobs of like value,
under each classification heading, can be seen, giving a horizontal
as well as a vertical check of acceptable order. Any job which
seems out of line compared with the other jobs surrounding it,
should be re-checked to ensure that no errors have been made in the
job analysis and assessment.

39

If the assessment is still felt to be correct, it should be removed temporarily from the board until the grading has been completed. It is rare to find more than a few jobs which require this treatment and, assuming relatively sound assessment, the reasons for their apparent misplacement can usually be found. For example, a job which has once been very easy or very difficult—but whose content over the years has changed—often appears at first glance to be out of line. Another common cause is where the title indicates a craft or highly specialised job but the actual work done does not require such expertise, for example, 'carpenter/joiner' who spends his time on odd jobs requiring little or no real skill. At the managerial level some job titles do not necessarily reflect responsibilities.

Selecting the Appropriate Number of Job Grades

Once the scrutiny has been completed the next step is to consider the number of different grades required. This will vary according to the range of jobs being evaluated in the application, but two points should be borne in mind. Firstly, if there are a large number of grades it is less easy for people to see real differences in the content of jobs in adjacent grades, and this leads both to unnecessary arguments and to feelings of unfairness. Secondly, at shop floor levels a large number of different grades can result in lack of mobility between jobs, and continuous attempts to leap-frog into higher grades. In hourly paid job evaluation schemes, if flexibility, on a day-to-day basis, is to be maintained and significant differences in job content recognised and rewarded, then, *on average*, a minimum of four and a maximum of six separate grades is usually required.

For managerial applications the small organisation will probably find that some six to eight grades will meet their requirements for all non-manual jobs: the medium-to-larger organisation is likely to require some eight to twelve grades, and the very large organisation with a wide range of activities will probably require a still greater number of grades if they wish to introduce a single structure for all their managerial jobs. In such cases there is an alternative way of dealing with this, which is to have a number of different functional structures, such as research & development, production, marketing, etc. The question of the relative merits of a single payment structure versus multiple payment structures is obviously important for an organisation. Apart from considerations of size and range of functions there may be policy, administrative or labour market reasons for wishing to introduce a number of different payment structures into an organisation. This is discussed in Chapter V. If an organisation chooses to have multiple payment structures, the guidance already given in terms of the number of grades required within any single structure is still relevant.

Criteria for Determining Where Grade Lines Should be Drawn
The devising of job grade lines is not a scientific process, and the criteria for doing so must be set in terms of common sense and ultimate acceptability of the results. Earlier in this chapter, we suggested that jobs be classified into like groups of activity and under each activity ranked in descending order of job value or scores. At this stage it is helpful to look both at the final rank order within each classification and identify:

> natural breaks in the rank order scores;
> jobs that are already interchangeable;
> job areas where greater flexibility of labour is required;
> jobs which form an acceptable and natural ladder of promotion;
> groups of jobs with common features such as educational or technical pre-requisites, duration of training or common skills;
> groups of jobs that have certain common sub-characteristics rated at the same levels;
> where job content is likely to change considerably in the short or medium term due to work study or technological changes;
> pattern of distribution of job skills.

This last point can be important in determining the shape of the grading structure for shop floor personnel. Over recent years the use of work study together with technological changes has led to a widening of the gap between demands of many groups of jobs. In general terms, whilst skill demands have increased for many craft workers and for some semi-skilled groups, for others they have decreased considerably.

Shape of Grade Structure
In analytical methods of job evaluation, natural break points for the grade structure often show up in gaps between job scores. In such cases the old concept of setting up grades of equal ranges of points values, i.e. on a straight line relationship, may be unrealistic. The shape of the grade structure may have to curve upwards and have unequal ranges of values within each grade. This is illustrated in figures 15 and 16, where job scores are plotted against money in the form of a scattergram.

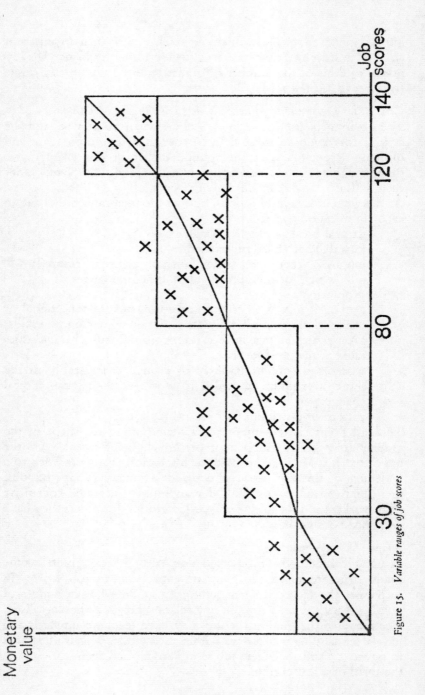

Figure 15. *Variable ranges of job scores*

42

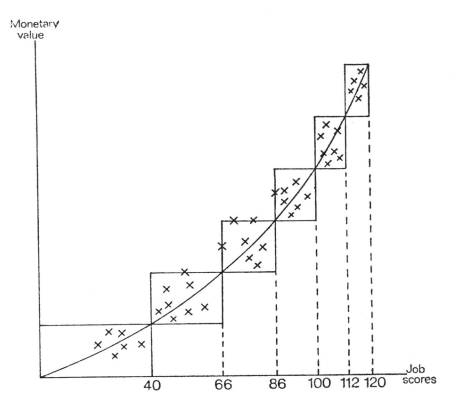

Figure 16. *Decreasing ranges of job scores*

Definition of Grades

So far criteria have been set up for identifying the areas in which grade lines might be drawn. Tentative grade ranges can now be set according to the shape of the emerging structure. At this stage the grade lines are tentative, since they can be moved up and down within a limited range, according to the definitions of the kinds of jobs which can be grouped together. It is useful now to specify the main features of each grade. An illustration of grade definitions for shop floor jobs is given on the following page.

43

Grade I: *Multi-Craft Jobs*
Jobs falling within this grade will require a basic
craft apprenticeship for a minimum period of 3 years,
plus the subsequent acquisition of a second basic
skill, e.g. mechanical and electrical. Points range
around 300–350.

Grade II: *Single Craft Jobs*
Jobs falling within this grade will require a basic
craft apprenticeship for a minimum period of 3 years.
They will have been rated at the top level (if points
assessment specify e.g. 7-10 points.) for knowledge
required and for at least two other mental factors.
Points range *around* 255-299.

. . .   .

Grade VI: *General Service Jobs*
Jobs falling within this grade will require up to 2-3
days' job training (excluding induction training) to
reach competent performance. Points range *around*
100–120.

So far the grading of the structure has been based on considerations
of organisation requirements and on the factual information thrown
up by the results of the job assessment programme. Before the structure can be finalised we have to put a price on each grade and
calculate both the degree of overpayment involved, and the incidence
of change in the earnings and relative status of individual job holders.
Thus at this stage the grade lines are tentatively stated as being
'around' certain points ranges.

PRICING THE BASE RATE STRUCTURE
There are two aspects to the pricing of grades: firstly, the setting
of payment levels and, secondly, the allocation of precise amounts
of money to each grade. In general terms this means taking into
account such factors as:
the level of base rates for similar jobs in other organisations;
the costs of introducing the new structure including dealing
with relative over- and under-payment:
the extent of change in relative job status and earnings both
immediately and in the long term.

Survey of Comparable Pay Rates in Other Organisations

The next step is to see how closely the general levels of base rate payment fit the general market values for similar jobs. Organisations who keep an eye on their recruitment and labour turnover figures by occupation will, to some extent, already know whether their payment levels and systems are adequate to recruit and retain the labour force they require. Similarly, they will already know which occupations are particularly vulnerable. For hourly paid jobs sources of comparison can be found in the Department of Employment and Productivity's labour statistics, from Employers' Federations, and by obtaining information from other organisations locally and/or within the appropriate industry in other regions: the Institute of Office Management regularly publishes statistics on clerical salaries, and there are several executive salary surveys carried out by institutions such as the BIM, professional associations and consultant bodies. When approaching other companies or institutions to obtain comparable information, job titles themselves can be misleading. Therefore it is necessary to select a number of jobs from the total range under consideration and to specify their content briefly in writing. The jobs selected should be representative of the different grades established by job evaluation and of the different specialisations or work activities involved. It is also important to state the actual wages data required by specifying and defining each separate element of pay on which information is being sought. Once this comparison has been completed, the organisation can assess whether its general level of base rate payments is adequate and establish its desired level. The next stage is to go back to the grades established by job evaluation and to cost out a number of alternative base pay rates within this general level.

Costing and Finalising the Structure

It is now necessary to obtain an overall picture of what these alternative pay rates, as applied to the tentative grade structure of jobs already devised, will mean in terms of cost and the extent of change to the existing structure of job rate relationships. This can best be seen by drawing a scattergram as in figure 14, but this time showing the tentative grade lines. This is illustrated in figure 17 where, again, job evaluated scores are plotted against present basic rates in pence per hour.

45

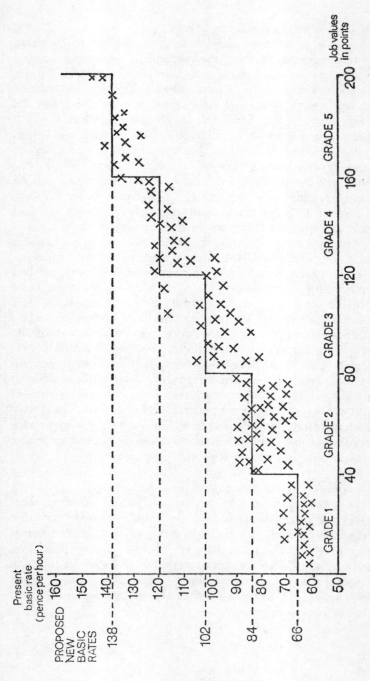

Figure 17. *Scattergram to show proposed new basic rates*

46

This figure is based on the assumption that management has decided on a five-grade structure with equal grade ranges of 40 points and equal payment differentials between each. The scattergram shows how alternative B of three possible sets of hourly rates (see table below) can be plotted: other alternatives can be plotted in the same way.

Alternative: (pence per hour)	A	B	C
Grade I	60	66	72
Grade II	78	84	90
Grade III	96	102	108
Grade IV	114	120	126
Grade V	132	138	144

From this scattergram we now see:
- (a) the proposed grade structure as represented by the horizontal ladder;
- (b) jobs which are at present relatively underpaid (those below the ladder);
- (c) jobs which are at present relatively overpaid (those above the ladder).

Scattergrams would then be drawn for alternatives A and C and a comparison made of the incidences of over- and under-payment in terms of the numbers of people involved and the cost of bringing all job rates into line with their new grade payment according to the job evaluation results.

So far we have discussed the pricing of the structure in terms of allocating a single rate of payment to each grade. However, ranges of payment, usually designed to permit discretionary merit payment between a minimum and a maximum, may also be introduced. Practice varies widely in the construction of ranges, but the two main types are discrete or overlapping. The use of ranges of payment, particularly overlapping ranges, is more common in building salary structures than in building a range structure for hourly paid personnel.

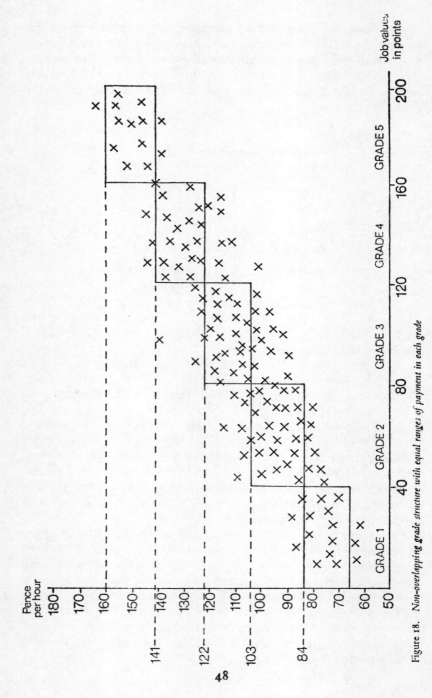

Figure 18. *Non-overlapping grade structure with equal ranges of payment in each grade*

48

Where an organisation wishes to introduce a range of payment for each grade, the scattergram should be drawn in terms of grade boxes. Figure 18 illustrates a 'discrete' or non-overlapping grade structure with equal ranges of payment for each grade. The payment ranges are:

grade	pence per hour
I	66 to 84
II	85 to 103
III	104 to 122
IV	123 to 141
V	142 to 160

Figure 19 (overleaf) illustrates an overlapping grade structure with increasing ranges of payment. Here it is evident that:
    (a) jobs which fall within each grade box are *relatively* in the correct pay relationships as established by job evaluation;
    (b) jobs above the grade boxes are, relative to their assessments, overpaid;
    (c) those below are relatively underpaid.
Once a number of alternative payment structures have been devised, it is essential to cost out the extent of over- and under-payment before finalising the structure for publication and/or negotiation.

The Need to Assess the Incidence of Job Grade and Earnings Changes
Where at first glance the degree of relative over- and under-payment seems reasonable, it is essential to obtain further data on the number of people in each job and the cost of bringing their present pay into line with the new proposals. It is usual in introducing a job evaluation scheme these days to start by giving a guarantee that no basic rates will be reduced. There are a number of ways of dealing with overpayment such as buying it out with a lump sum or changing the job content to bring the job demands up to the level of present payment. This is a matter of policy and is dealt with more fully below.
If a proposed structure does not prove acceptable on the grounds that the overpaid jobs involve too high a proportion of the work force, higher rates of payment can be plotted to see whether this gives a more acceptable result. The alternative might be to alter the grade lines or increase the number of grades, especially if there are clear signs of a clustering of overpaid jobs on the borderline of the next higher grades.

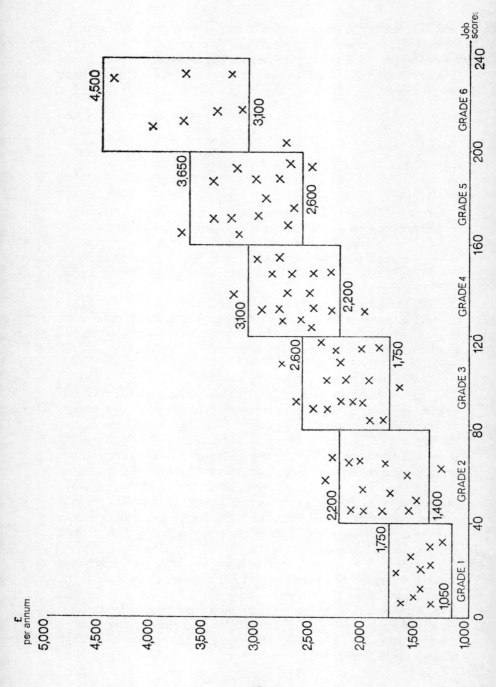

When a number of cost calculations have been made in this manner, the problem of the incidence of changes in relative job status should be examined. If too many people are involved in change and/or there is too great a move away from traditional job relationships, the new structure is unlikely to be acceptable. In such cases management must weigh up the cost involved in making the structure more acceptable against such possible effects as a fall in morale, increased staff or labour turnover, protracted negotiations, withdrawal of co-operation and restrictions on output. It is often cheaper, in the long run, to select grades with a lower incidence of disturbance but a slightly higher initial cost in terms of payment levels.

Policy on Over- and Under-Payment
Before leaving the question of pricing the pay structure, let us look at the question of dealing with over- and under-payment in more detail. There are few organisations of any size that will not find some jobs which in terms of the job evaluation are under- or overpaid. It is all too easy to say there is no problem in underpayment, and indeed some organisations immediately bring these jobs up to the right payment level without further analysis. Before doing this, however, management should carefully analyse such factors as performance levels, labour or staff turnover rates and difficulties of recruitment. More than once, an organisation has found that past underpayment, over a long time, has resulted in both poor quality of staff and low performance levels. Simply to push up the rate immediately would be uneconomic and some phasing of the increases, accompanied by retraining or changes in job methods or content, should be considered. Overpayment can be dealt with in a number of different ways, such as:

(a) altering job content to make greater use of higher skill levels, thus bringing the job value into line;
(b) buying out the overpayment with a lump sum of money;
(c) phasing out the overpayment over a period of time, say 12 months;
(d) a mixture of the above two methods;
(e) making a personal allowance to individual job holders until a job of a higher range of skill becomes available;
(f) agreeing that overpaid jobs will not, or only marginally, participate in general annual increases until the overpayment is absorbed.

Sometimes an analysis of personal data, i.e. age, length of service, etc., can be useful. In some situations, especially where merit rating systems have been used in the past, a correlation can be found between overpayment and length of service. A similar correlation can often be found in management salaries where annual increments in salary are given on an across-the-board basis. Where this is so, organisations have found it to their advantage to introduce a long-service payment which, together with the new rate, avoids an active loss of pay. This is a form of buying out, but it usually creates goodwill in that personnel can feel that the organisation recognises their stability and service. Which method or mixture of methods is used will clearly be dependent on the level of overpayment and the incidence of it amongst different groups of employees.

In hourly paid and other unionised applications it is highly desirable to discuss these different methods of dealing with anomalies and jointly agree the policy before negotiation of the final rate structure.

CHAPTER IV

APPLYING JOB EVALUATION

We have discussed what job evaluation is and the various ways in which the results can be used to build a payment structure. This chapter is concerned with more general considerations in applying job evaluation. For convenience we recall the four main phases of work:

1. Preparatory
2. Analysis and assessment
3. Building and pricing the structure
4. Negotiation, implementation and control

PHASE I: PREPARATORY

During this phase an organisation is involved in three main activities, namely making policy decisions, procedural arrangements, and undertaking certain initial preparatory work and wage analysis.

Policy Decisions

Once the decision to carry out job evaluation has been made, there are a number of policy matters which must be decided before the evaluation process can begin. The major decisions are:

1. The range of jobs to be evaluated.
2. The choice of method of job evaluation to be used.
3. The extent to which employees are to be involved in the evaluation process.
4. How to deal with the overpayments which arise as a result of the job evaluation.
5. Whether or not to use outside consultants (discussed in Chapter VI).
6. In a large organisation, with geographically dispersed units, whether there is to be one unified payment structure or whether local structures will be introduced (discussed in Chapter VI).
7. Decisions relating to the type of grading structure which the organisation wishes to introduce, e.g. whether more or fewer grades are desired than exist at present (see Chapter III).

It is important in setting objectives in relation to the grading structure which will stem from the job evaluation, to take into account the organisation's policy on its total remuneration system, i.e. whether or not it wishes to use payment by results schemes, partially or in whole, and what other elements of pay are required. Further, in finalising decisions on the number of grades required it is important, as we have already pointed out, that the organisation gives full consideration to its needs for labour mobility, especially as they may alter in the light of planned technological changes.

The above matters not dealt with in other chapters are discussed below.

1. *Range of jobs to be evaluated*
   It is difficult to envisage a situation where an analytical method of job evaluation can be used to evaluate all jobs in an organisation 'from managing director to tea-boy' in one scheme, since definition of characteristics, and their relative significance, is unlikely to be common to all levels. Thus, although the same basic method may be used, different schemes will be required for the various levels of work in an organisation. Decisions are therefore required as to the cut-off points for each level. For example, are supervisors and junior technical staff to be covered in one scheme, or separate schemes?

2. *Choice of method*
   The choice of method will be influenced by the following main considerations:
   (a) the advantages and disadvantages of the various systems as described in Chapter II;
   (b) the time and personnel available to carry out the exercise —every job evaluation exercise is time consuming but some methods are faster than others;
   (c) the industrial relations background and the degree of co-operation which can be achieved (consideration must also be given to the extent of the need for management and the unions to be able to satisfy employees that all aspects of their jobs have been carefully considered—if this need is great an analytical system will be required);
   (d) the basic objectives of management, i.e. the extent to which they wish to modify or completely revise the existing structure;

(e) the uses to which the data collected during the evaluation will be put (e.g. are its results to be used for purposes other than revising the wage structure, such as better selection, improved training arrangements, etc?);

(f) the type of jobs being evaluated—are they all in one function, or across a number of functions?;

(g) the size of the undertaking.

3. *Extent of employee involvement*

It is technically possible to carry out a job evaluation exercise without employee participation to the stage where negotiations take place on the pay for each grade. Most organisations, however, feel that they would be missing a major opportunity to improve and develop their industrial relations if they did not involve trade unions and employees to some extent. There are good reasons for holding this view because, in the final analysis, the success or failure of job evaluation depends on its acceptance and understanding by the employees affected. This acceptance is more likely if the groups affected feel that they have been involved.

Each organisation must make up its mind as to the extent of employee involvement it wishes to encourage and this will be dependent on the general industrial relations background and the management and trade union attitudes to job evaluation. There are normally three degrees of involvement practised:

(a) involvement in writing job descriptions but nothing else;

(b) involvement in job description writing and on the evaluation committee or evaluation process either as evaluators or observers;

(c) involvement from the beginning, including choice of scheme, factors to be used and, where appropriate to the scheme, involvement at the weighting stage and possibly in the drawing of grade lines.

4. *Dealing with over-payment*

Employees will expect management to state at an early stage how it proposes to deal with any jobs out of line which will arise when the evaluation is implemented. Normally, management give an undertaking stating the principle that no employee will lose money as a result of the evaluation, but stress that the way in which anomalies will be dealt with cannot be discussed until the job evaluation results are known.

Procedural Arrangements

Before the evaluation can begin, a series of important procedural decisions must be taken. Among these are:

1. The appointment of a co-ordinator for the exercise. This will normally be the individual who will be responsible for maintaining the new wage structure after it has been implemented.
2. The appointment of an evaluation committee. Normally it is wise to appoint people who, between them, have wide experience of the range of jobs being evaluated. In some organisations provision is made for *ad hoc* membership of the committee by departmental managers when jobs in their departments are being evaluated. Although this has the advantage of bringing detailed knowledge of these jobs to the attention of the evaluators, there is also a danger that some individuals may use the occasion for 'special pleading'.
3. A decision as to whether the same committee will deal with both the evaluation and the drawing up of a new pay structure. Practice varies widely according to the amount of trade union involvement, size of firm, seniority of the evaluation committee, etc.
4. The frequency of meeting of the committee. The aim should be to complete the evaluation in the shortest possible time, as undue length leads to frustration, suspicion and dissatis-faction on the part of those whose jobs are being evaluated. A full-time committee is desirable; three days per week is the minimum recommended.
5. Whether the organisation is sufficiently large to justify the appointment of a hierarchy of committees. This will speed up the work, especially where units are geographically dispersed, but if a hierarchy is used, special attention must be paid to maintaining consistency between the committees.
6. The procedure for writing job descriptions. In small or-ganisations it is usual for the committee to write the job description. In large organisations special job analysts are normally appointed and trained to carry out the work. It is normal, especially with managerial jobs, for job holders

to agree the descriptions of their jobs.

7. The communication procedures to be adopted to inform employees of management's intentions regarding job evaluation. We refer to this aspect in more detail under Phase II.

Initial Work

The initial work required includes the setting up of a job identification programme and carrying out an analysis of existing wages or salaries. If the initial investigation shows that the organisational framework requires rationalisation, this must be done before job identification is carried out.

1. *Job identification*

   The purpose of a job identification programme is to ensure that employees feel that significant differences between one job (or series of tasks) and another will be recognised during the evaluation process. Often jobs comprising very different tasks carry the same title, or jobs with different titles are in reality very similar. Obviously, the number of jobs identified has implications both for the length of time required to carry out the evaluation exercise, and for the number of people needed to make the assessments or write the job descriptions.

2. *Wage analysis*

   In order that the total programme of reforming the wages or salary structure can proceed smoothly, an analysis of the present position needs to be initiated during Phase I as this takes time, and the data should be available by the time the evaluation work is completed so that the grading work can proceed without delay. This analysis will include the following data, broken down by occupational groups:

   length of service of employees

   age of employees

   present basic rates

   piecework earnings, if appropriate

   all other elements of payment such as merit money, shift allowances, etc.

level of overtime payments

fringe benefits

PHASE II: ANALYSIS AND ASSESSMENT

Having discussed the preliminary decisions which must be made, we can now outline the steps involved in carrying out job evaluation. Although these steps are described consecutively, some of them will, in practice, be concurrent, and the details of each step will vary widely according to the job evaluation scheme used and the size of organisation. For convenience we list the steps before amplifying them:

informing employees

selecting and training job analysts or assessors

devising the framework of the evaluation method chosen and testing the scheme

evaluating the mass of jobs

checking the rank order for anomalies

Informing Employees

All employees, including supervisors, like to feel that:

the method of evaluation is logical and fair;

all jobs are to be evaluated on the same basis;

the jobs will be evaluated by people who understand their content.

Unless it is properly explained, the introduction of job evaluation evokes suspicion among employees who may feel that it is their their individual performance which is being investigated rather than their jobs. Thus, whatever the degree of employee involvement decided upon, every organisation carrying out job evaluation needs to communicate its intentions to all those affected. Methods of communication within firms vary widely; what is essential is that the methods chosen are effective. Often a series of meetings are held, including meeting with managers and supervisors in those cases where only hourly paid employees are being evaluated. At these meetings the intentions of the exercise should be made clear, and the methods to be used in carrying out the evaluation explained. In large organisations only shop stewards are likely to be present, but in small organisations, or where only small groups are affected, the employees themselves should be invited to attend. As most job evaluation exercises take some time, it is important to remember to give a progress report about mid-way through the application.

Selecting and Training of Job Analysts or Assessors

Whether there is to be a single panel of assessors, or a central panel with several teams of assessors, it is important to select and train them with care for the success of job evaluation will depend on the results of their work. The following are some of the more important attributes which assessors should possess:

the ability to undertake detailed work;

open mindedness, i.e. willingness to accept new views;

the ability to ask detailed questions without upsetting the listener;

the ability to listen to, and perceive the significance of, the answers to his questions;

if possible, a wide acquaintance of the type of work and jobs being analysed.

In some situations it may be unwise to second work study personnel to job evaluation work, even though they often meet the above requirements. The reason for this is that, particularly when the jobs of hourly paid staff are being assessed, employees may erroneously assume that job evaluation is being used to change work standards.

The training of the analysts or assessors should cover the following:

the method of job evaluation being used and why it has been chosen;

how to interview and obtain information on jobs, and the procedures to be followed in recording the information so that consistency is maintained— normally, the facts relating to each sub-factor are recorded on a specially prepared form;

detailed acquaintance with the benchmark jobs in order

that each assessor has a common framework for
assessment.

In order to ensure that all assessors are working on a common calibration there is a need for close supervision and checking of the first jobs assessed by each assessor.

Devising the Framework and Testing the Scheme

Once the method of carrying out the evaluation has been chosen, the way the job evaluation scheme is to be developed must be devised in detail. For example, if a classification method has been selected, the number of grades must be decided and a clear definition appropriate for each grade must be written. If an analytical scheme is to be used, the factors and sub-factors must be selected and the rating scale decided.

A number of benchmark jobs, whose relationships one to the other are unlikely to be disputed, should be selected, described in detail, and evaluated using the tentative scheme. The job description is a vital document as it provides, in most schemes, the major evidence on which the evaluation is made. It must, therefore, be carefully prepared (see Appendix I). This trial run provides the opportunity for testing the validity of the characteristics selected and allows for tentative weightings to be drawn up. It is at this stage that modifications can be made in order to achieve an acceptable final result.

At this stage a manual of how to assess jobs should be written for the use of the assessors. The manual should include sections on the method of evaluation being used, definitions of the factors and sub-factors selected, and the procedures to be used while carrying out the assessment of jobs.

Evaluating the Mass of Jobs

For most schemes this step involves writing job descriptions for all the other jobs, though the profile method dispenses with full job descriptions except for the benchmark jobs. The job identification programme will be finalised at this stage to ensure that no jobs have been missed, and that the same job, masquerading under different names, is not assessed twice.

Planning the work of the analysts and assessors is essential at this stage. Unless this is well done, major delays will occur in the total programme, arising from the analysts waiting for people to give information about jobs.

During the analysis or assessment it is usual for the analysts to work in pairs. It is always necessary that they discuss what they are doing with the supervisor and shop steward in a department before carrying out their work. With hourly paid jobs the greater the amount of time spent on the shop floor, as opposed to an office, the more accurate the analysis is likely to be. It is also important for analysts to explain to everyone concerned what they are doing and why they are doing it. In this way people can gain a greater understanding of, and trust in, the evaluation method being used.

An evaluation committee will now evaluate the jobs using the job descriptions and the benchmark jobs as guides. The actual process of evaluation will vary with the scheme used as shown in the figure 13, but the outcome will be the same—a rank order for all jobs.

Checking the Rank Order for Jobs out of Line
The rank order is now carefully scrutinised to identify those jobs which appear to be out of line with their expected position. These jobs will be checked to determine that the job was correctly identified, described properly, and that no mistakes were made during the evaluation.

PHASE III: BUILDING AND PRICING THE STRUCTURE
Building and pricing the structure has been dealt with in detail in the previous chapter. Here we only are concerned with who should carry out the work involved which consists of:

         grading
         pricing and costing

Grading is sometimes carried out by a special team of top managers, or in some organisations by the same group which was responsible for the evaluation of the jobs. Practice varies on whether trade union representatives should be involved in the grading work.

Pricing and costing, however, cannot be a joint management/union exercise, because the results are subject to negotiation. As the money to be paid for each grade is tied up with the organisation's general policy on wages or salaries, it is usual to set up a group of senior managers to determine the suggested new rates and how to deal with any anomalies. This group is often composed of the individuals who will form a wages/salary committee responsible for the maintenance of the scheme, though they will have a team of assessors to help them.

When job evaluation is used in conjunction with labour utilisation negotiations, or comprehensive productivity bargaining, anomalies may be discussed jointly with unions. Where this happens, discussion will normally range round how job content can be changed to utilise more of the available skills of the people performing work.

PHASE IV: NEGOTIATION, IMPLEMENTATION AND CONTROL
The essential features of this phase are:

> preparing a written manual which describes the method of job evaluation introduced, defines the characteristics if an analytical scheme has been used, and lists the key or benchmark jobs;
> drafting an agreement which sets out clearly the ranges and rates of payment for each grade, and refers to the maintenance procedures;
> laying down review procedures both for new jobs and for dealing with existing jobs which have changed their content;
> setting up a committee for regular review and control of the new wage or salary structure.

It is not appropriate in this guide to discuss the negotiation of agreements with unions other than to say that a company's normal negotiating procedures should be used. Trade union fears that too close an involvement in Phase II of the evaluation will tie their hands during negotiation can be more imaginary than real because the negotiation stage is quite separate from the investigation one.

There will be a number of appeals against the grading of certain jobs. These should be dealt with rapidly, using a procedure which is agreed between management and unions, and which can be clearly understood by all concerned.

Before considering the ways in which successful maintenance procedures should be established, it is useful to examine the usual causes of decay of job evaluation schemes. These include:

> failure to take immediate account of significant changes in job content: regular vetting of contents of jobs against job descriptions is therefore essential;
> an inflexible attitude in interpreting the scheme;
> failure to make revisions following organisational changes;
> lack of management support;
> allowing other components of the pay structure to become so large that the evaluated differentials have little significance;
> insufficient time available for regular review of scheme;
> loss of employee acceptance, possibly because so many cases have been treated as exceptions that faith in the scheme has diminished.

A well-written and definitive manual is the basis of successful maintenance, for it serves as the authority against which consistency can be maintained and queries answered. Without such a manual the basis on which certain key decisions were taken during the implementation phase are soon forgotten, so that new decisions would be likely to be inconsistent with previous practice.

For maintenance and control there is a need to set up a committee which can deal with changes which take place in job content. In this connection it is important to remember that minor alternations in job content are always taking place, and the review committee needs to be careful to ensure that apparent changes in job content really have significance in terms of job demand. Their task will be made easier if a job evaluation system has been used which ensures that only really significant differences in job demand have been considered during the original assessment.

As new jobs arise, management will need to propose a grade for them. The starting point should be the writing of a job description and its theoretical assessment by the review committee. This assessment forms the basis for agreeing a provisional grading and normally stands for an agreed period. At the end of this period, when the job has settled down, a new evaluation of it should take place. Besides dealing with appeals, job changes and new jobs, the review committee should be concerned with regular overall audits of the wage or salary structure. This involves collecting and examining data on the number of grade changes which have been made since the last review, any changes in labour mix which are taking place, and identifying the extent of which jobs have gradually drifted up to a higher grade than that originally established. They should also examine the organisation's wage and salaries movements in relation to similar changes in the area and within the industry. Finally they need to look ahead and be aware of the likely effects of technological changes on the overall wages or salary structure.

CHAPTER V

MULTIPLE PAY STRUCTURES AND MARKET GROUPS

Reference has been made in Chapter III to the use of multiple structures in order to establish more effective relationships for homogeneous groups of jobs. Multiple-structure approaches have also been found useful when establishing the financial value of job evaluation results, particularly where organisations want to ensure adequate comparability with rates paid elsewhere for similar skills. In this chapter some of the implications of establishing a pay structure in relation to the labour market are discussed, as well as some approaches to multiple structures.

The Labour Market

The basic difference between pay structuring based on job evaluation, compared with the absence of job evaluation, is in the way that decisions are made.

Without job evaluation, decisions on pay are continually made usually by a number of people—supervisors, managers, personnel specialists, wage negotiators; and these decisions are usually based on their judgment as to the 'value' of a particular individual or group of employees.

With job evaluation, attention is taken away from the person performing the job to the job itself. The relative relationships between jobs are determined by the application of uniform criteria and also decisions on base rates or pay scales can be made with a comprehensive unified approach.

Nonetheless, the fundamental question of how much to pay is not determined by job evaluation. Job evaluation may show that Job X should be paid more than Job Y, but not what either should be paid in actual terms.

The development of pay structures comes down to a basic question of what rate or scale should be attached to a particular job. The simple answer must be: whatever is required to permit recruitment and retention of employees with the requisite skills to perform the job. This puts the determination of rates in the context of supply and demand, which in some ways is more satisfactory in theory than in practice, since the labour market is an imperfect one. Nevertheless, some organisations feel that a labour market approach is the only thing available to work with, and organisations clearly need to take account of the general level of payment within the community for similar jobs or skills.

The labour market is difficult to work with because it is subject to a number of influences. Some of the difficulties encountered in working with the concept of a labour market are due to the following:

1. Labour is both the product and the seller, and therefore does not respond in the same way as other commodities.

2. Labour is affected by many other values in addition to money, such as security, achievement, social esteem, etc.

3. Labour is not always mobile and free to change jobs, nor always well informed as to its value on the market.

4. Labour rates are frequently strongly influenced by trade union negotiation, and may be subject to Government policy.

5. The market value of labour is not precise. A survey of organisations to determine the rate of pay for ostensibly the same job will produce a range of payments that may be quite wide. Some of this dispersion may be due to imprecise comparisons of jobs and skills. However, a range of payments rather than a common rate is the best that can be expected.

In spite of the difficulties of assessing the labour market, employers should take account of rates paid by other employers for similar work. Great care must be taken in gathering such information, and discretion used in its analysis. Assessing the appropriate relationship for a structure in relation to the community market values requires careful judgment. In addition to considering the relationship of the current structure to the rest of the community, one needs to assess such things as the job security, opportunity for advancement and benefits provided by the organisation, as compared to others.

A further difficulty in assessing the labour market by checking rates with other organisations is that rates may not be reflective of earnings. This is particularly true of hourly paid jobs where piecework and associated bonuses are involved. In this case comparisons of average earnings for common periods (e.g. 40 hours) is more valid. Even then some knowledge of the make-up of earnings and the incentive system is required.

Multiple Structures

In few organisations is it possible to have a single pay structure, particularly if the organisation contains a variety of labour categories such as dayworkers, pieceworkers, clerical staff, technical staff and management personnel.

There are a number of reasons for this:

1. Different payment systems (daywork, piecework, salary) often apply according to categories of employees, and are difficult to rationalise into a single pay structure.
2. Conditions of employment, such as overtime premiums, holiday calculations and benefits often differ according to categories of employees, and these make a single structure difficult to operate.
3. Various categories of employees are normally represented by different trade unions. If rates are to be negotiated or subsequently affected by general increase negotiations, then a structure that cuts across the interests of more than one negotiating body will be difficult to maintain.
4. Jobs in different categories (e.g. manual and staff) have such different characteristics that it is difficult to find criteria that will permit effective evaluation for a single structure.
5. Market values for categories of staff move independently, for example, as between manual and staff, clerical and technical.

For the above reasons, some separation of pay structures is required in virtually all organisations. As a basic point of departure the following separate structures are suggested:

Manual jobs:	piecework structure
	daywork structure
Staff jobs:	clerical structure
	technical structure
	management structure

Variations on this will very much depend on the nature of the organisation and the trade union negotiating arrangements currently in effect.

Market Group Concept

A further refinement to the above mentioned approach to multiple structures is called the 'market group concept'. In this approach jobs are grouped together which meet two criteria:

1. Jobs in which the recruitment qualifications overlap and amongst which employees can readily move by extending or adapting their skills.
2. Jobs in which a change in the market value for one will produce a similar effect on all.

As examples from various levels in an organisation, the following would be separated into market groups:

> Engineers from Accountants
> Draughtsmen from Laboratory Technicians
> Secretaries from General Clerical
> Material Handlers from Machinists

It is argued that job evaluation over a long period can only be effectively maintained by grading within market groups but not across them. This is because market values change relatively between groups, though their relative positions remain the same within groups. Thus a separate structure is developed for each market group.

While the market group approach is not widely adopted in its fullest extension, there are examples where it is used. Although not necessarily done for explicit reasons of a market approach, it can be argued that any separation of pay structures in some way recognises the existence of independent market pressures.

Local or National Structures

Those organisations operating in more than one location have an additional decision to make in respect of single or multiple structures. Examples and supporting arguments can be found for the two alternatives—the same structure for all locations, or different structures for each.

Those supporting the same structure across locations would argue that it is administratively easier, simplifies employee transfers between locations, and is thought to be more equitable. On the other hand, rates do vary between different locations within the country and as long as this persists the individual organisation may find it more appropriate to establish separate structures based on compatibility with rates paid in each.

As there is no rule in this respect the individual organisation must make its own decision based on policy, cost and recognition of the extent of the area from which employees are normally recruited.

Conclusion

While the analysis and assessment of jobs is the most time consuming aspect of job evaluation, the determination of the financial valuation to apply to its results is the more complex part of the work. As there is no absolute criterion for the determination of pay, and practice varies widely, no single approach to pay structuring can be recommended. However, if the job evaluation exercise is to remain viable over a long period, it must be capable of responding to changing values. It may be found that the adoption of multiple structures is the most practical way of providing this flexibility.

CHAPTER VI

OTHER CONSIDERATIONS

The reader will have noticed that we have avoided recommending one method of job evaluation as being technically superior to others. The reason for this hesitancy is that all methods may have advantages in certain situations. Some are rapid and easy to apply, others are possibly of more lasting value but require greater effort to introduce. Each organisation must make up its mind which method is suitable for its own circumstances. In general, however, it is safe to say that analytical methods will give a more effective result than non-analytical methods.

The way in which job evaluation is introduced and implemented is of major significance and of greater importance for the well-being of an organisation than the technical merits of a particular system. Thus, those methods of application which encourage involvement of those whose jobs are being evaluated, and/or their representatives, and at the same time maintain consistency and ease of maintenance, are to be preferred.

The Use of Consultants

Of the various reasons why consultants may be used, three are common enough to be discussed here. First, the task of revising the wage structure may be so involved that management decides that it needs outside specialist assistance. Secondly, the internal industrial relations background may be such that management feels that the results of the evaluation will be more acceptable if independent specialists have played a major role during the evaluation exercise. Thirdly, the organisation may not have sufficient trained staff available to carry through the evaluation, and may feel that the use of consultants on a temporary basis is cheaper than recruiting suitable men to the permanent establishment.

The use of outside consultants does not relieve management of responsibility. When the job evaluation has been completed, and the new wage structure introduced, management will have to maintain the system. If this maintenance is to be done well, the staff responsible will need to understand thoroughly all the steps and decisions which were taken during the introductory period. Thus members of staff will be required to assist the consultants either full time or part time according to the role they are assigned in the total job evaluation exercise. Certainly the use of consultants should not be viewed as a means of shedding managerial responsibility, but rather as a method of carrying out the work involved more rapidly and more economically.

Pre-Requisites for Success
We do not know a guaranteed recipe for a successful job evaluation scheme, but there are certain ingredients for success, the neglect of which can result in an unacceptable scheme.

The first need is for firm management commitment and understanding at all levels of management of the reasons why job evaluation is being introduced. Without this understanding no lasting benefit can emerge from the time and effort invested.

A second need is to ensure that the extent of participation in the job evaluation exercise, on the part of those who will be affected by it, is in line with their expectations. By this we mean that, in general, people wish to feel that they have made a positive contribution to the process through which their ultimate pay packet will be determined.

Third, it is no use carrying out job evaluation unless a well thought out exercise in communication has been undertaken. People will be suspicious of the reasons why others are examining their jobs in detail unless they recognise and understand the need for such examination.

Fourth, the industrial relations climate should be such that the job evaluation work can be carried out in an objective manner.

Fifth, it is desirable to carry out some kind of organisation and methods check at all levels before introducing job evaluation. This at least ensures that jobs being evaluated exist in a sensible form. We know of cases where job evaluation has been very difficult to apply because the job holders had insufficiently defined duties or responsibilities. It is also desirable that no immediate major changes in organisation are about to take place which might call for a major re-evaluation programme.

Sixth, once the scheme has been established, it should be operated consistently. Appeals for special treatment of certain jobs for reasons which cannot be substantiated against the evaluation criteria should be firmly resisted. Arbitrary adjustments, if substantial in number, soon result in the collapse of the scheme, as it no longer meets the requirement of consistency and fairness. There is thus a need for a clear manual of procedures and a regular review of the scheme.

But perhaps the most important ingredient is that those being evaluated should have no doubts about management's sincerity. If they feel that management is using job evaluation as a cover for the introduction of new practices or techniques to which they are wholly opposed, then, however well-intentioned management may be, the exercise will fail.

The Relationship of Job Evaluation to the Total Personnel Policies of an Organisation

Essentially job evaluation is a fact-finding exercise. It is concerned with what is actually happening, not with what people think is happening. Although it is concerned with jobs and the way work is organised, this work has to be done by people. Job evaluation, therefore, has an important relationship to the total personnel policies in an organisation, for example, selection and training. Not only does it enable the exact requirements for each job to be more readily identified, but it also offers the opportunity for career progression through a grade structure to be introduced. Such a career progression requires for its success the introduction of appropriate appraisal and training schemes.

Perhaps the most significant relationship is in the field of industrial relations because well thought out and well conducted job evaluation offers the opportunity for developing and improving the industrial relations climate. The way in which communication is carried out, the amount of consultation and participation that takes place, and the manner in which subsequent negotiations are conducted, can all improve or worsen the existing industrial relations climate. One of the biggest potential advantages is that job evaluation offers an opportunity for the negotiations about the final wage or salary structure to be based on facts rather than opinions or fancies. This enables both sides to focus discussion on real points of difference, and not on misconceptions as to the true nature of the work being carried out.

Another great advantage is that, often for the first time, employees feel that management is taking the trouble to find out exactly what skills and knowledge they possess and the way in which they apply them. Good questioning during job interviewing, and the extent to which employees feel they have influenced the results, are major factors both in gaining final acceptability for the new wage structure, and in improving industrial relations. What is more, it provides both sides with the experience of completing successfully a joint task which may encourage them to tackle jointly the problems of entering into and completing an effective and comprehensive productivity bargain.

Trade Unions and Job Evaluation

Trade union policy on the degree of involvement they wish to have in carrying out a job evaluation varies considerably. Some unions wish no involvement whatsoever and others wish full involvement. Some unionists take the view that members' interests are best served by actively participating in the implementation of the scheme, serving on an assessment committee, and being fully involved. Other unionists take the opposite view; they believe that the danger of commitment to the system undermines the representative's ability to appeal against assessments that prove to be unacceptable to a group of his members. They prefer management to operate the scheme as a managerial responsibility, reserving to themselves the right to challenge and check. These are extreme positions between which various intermediate positions can be taken. (There are similar differences of view on the employers' side.) The one thing which is commonly required by unions, however, is full information about the system.

Management should assess the views of trade unions before committing themselves to a particular level of involvement. It should be remembered that views may vary as between craft and non-craft unions.

As major trade union involvement in job evaluation cannot be regarded as a 'once and for all' exercise, management should recognise that such major involvement, if a departure from previous practice, will almost inevitably lead to demands for further involvement in other areas which affect their work/payment arrangements. This is not necessarily a development to be regretted by management, as it can bring considerable improvements in productivity, but it does mean that they should possess the capacity to handle this kind of development if it takes place.

Many workers regard their status and esteem according to the grade in which their job has been placed, irrespective of the money being paid. This is often of considerable importance to craft workers, and can be important in relation to morale. Management should always try to devise schemes which show clear promotion lines.

In saying this we are making the point that management ought to analyse job evaluation results with a view to identifying jobs with similar basic skills which form a natural promotion ladder.

The changes in job content brought about by technological advances and the use of new approaches for managing and controlling a business have been accompanied by a considerable increase of white-collar workers in the private sectors of industry. The private sector is likely to have an increase in white-collar representation in the future, and this means that there is a need to involve their representatives in a salary application just as they would involve shop floor representatives.

Job Evaluation and Collective Bargaining
People are often very worried avout how job evaluation results will be affected by national agreements. Sometimes the criteria of how to deal with this are not altogether clear. It is relatively easy when the national agreement provides for a uniform percentage increase 'across the board', for then the increase can be paid on existing rates. Where the increase is expressed in monetary terms, e.g. 6d. 'across the board', the relationship between established grade payments alters and can cause difficulties. Greater difficulty arises when the increases are not uniform, for then dispute about the interpretation of a national agreement as it applies to particular jobs can and does arise. These problems should, of course, be foreseen, and procedures for dealing with them agreed on the introduction of the scheme.

The other point often raised is that an organisation's job evaluation scheme may cut across collective bargaining agreements at industry level. Certainly, there are dangers if an organisation pays no attention at all to the relevant national agreements or procedures, or to the effects of its own agreements on workers in other organisations in the same industry or service. It is important, in this as in other areas of collective bargaining, that the appropriate authorities in the unions concerned are consulted before local negotiators even enter into discussions that might lead to the introduction of job evaluation.

Conclusion
Job evaluation is not a panacea for all wage and salary problems. At best it is an *analytical* tool which will give management and unions more factual information about job content and job relationships. Even where a non-analytical method is used it will at least pin-point

the worst aspects of existing payment anomalies. What is most important is the way in which job evaluation is applied and its results used. It is essential that those people whose jobs are being evaluated understand the system and become involved in its application. This means that the planning work before the application must be thorough, and that it must include a sound programme of communications.

The analytical method of job evaluation, properly applied, will give an organisation the following benefits:

1. A basic wage or salary structure in which payment reflects job content and in which the grades of pay are derived from known and agreed facts rather than hunches.

2. Knowledge of how to relate other pay elements to that structure in such a way that total earnings do not completely erode the differentials established by job evaluation.

3. Sufficient detailed information about jobs to enable the total structure to be maintained in acceptably good order in the face of changes in job content or the introduction of new jobs.

4. A new wage or salary structure which is generally simple to operate and cheaper to administer in the long run.

5. Information which can lead to improvement in such areas as work structure, recruitment, selection and training.

6. If well applied, an improvement in management/employee relationships.

7. In collective bargaining situations, if jointly applied, it can lead to greater mutual understanding of each other's problems by both management and trade unions. Thus it can be the first step in improving formal industrial relations in an organisation.

It is benefits such as these that have led to the considerable increase in the use of job evaluation over recent years.

APPENDIX I

JOB DESCRIPTIONS

A job description is necessary to provide information for the analysis and evaluation of jobs. It is a report which outlines the duties, responsibilities and conditions applicable to the job under review. It is essentially a description of the job itself, and not of the individual who is performing the job.

Formats of job descriptions vary between companies, but they generally include the title of the job; a summary of its basic functions (i.e. why the job exists), duties and responsibilities; organisational relationships; limits of authority.

The preparation of job descriptions should follow a procedure which results in the most useful finished product available. A well-designed description is a valuable document for a number of purposes outside job evaluation, including:

> giving present employees a better understanding of their present jobs;

> the introduction of new employees to their jobs;

> assisting in recruitment, and in placing employees in jobs for which they are better suited;

> clarification of relationships between jobs, to avoid overlaps and gaps in responsibilities;

> assessment of performance by comparing the employee's achievements with the specified requirements of the job;

> training.

The programme for the preparation of job descriptions may conveniently be divided into four separate stages which may be briefly described as follows:

75

1. *Preparation*

   Firstly, at least one person needs to be nominated to undertake the duties of a job analyst which include analysing the jobs and writing descriptions. The job analyst should be a person with a good general knowledge of the company's or-ganisational structure and of the jobs affected. He should have an analytical approach to the subject, and be capable of separating facts from opinions. Furthermore, he must be able to gain the confidence of management and to obtain the co-operation of employees. Lastly, he must be able to keep sight of his objective, which is to produce concise job des-criptions. In small firms this could be a part-time job for a manager, or possibly the personnel officer if there is one.

   There are obvious advantages in allocating this job to a member of the staff who already has a good knowledge of the company's operations, although preliminary training may be needed in other aspects of the job. The person chosen should be able to devote his full attention to the job. As an alternative, consideration may be given to the engagement of a con-sultant with experience in this field or the recruitment of an experienced analyst from outside.

2. *Obtaining the Information*

   The analyist may obtain the required information on the contents of jobs by the use of the following techniques:

   (a) *Observation.* For jobs of a simple and repetitive nature adequate information may be obtained from first-hand observation of the jobs being performed. This may give a sufficiently clear picture of the working conditions, equipment used and skills required. Employees should, of course, be advised beforehand of the reasons for the analyst's visit, to avoid suspicion.

   Although all jobs should be observed, this technique alone is not sufficient for more complicated jobs or those of a diverse nature, e.g. clerical work.

   (b) *Interview.* To obtain the necessary information which is not available on observation, an interview with the job holder is appropriate. Interviews should be conducted in a relaxed atmosphere to encourage job holders to co-operate in discussing their jobs freely. The interview should be followed by a meeting with the job holder's superior to verify the information given and to check any doubtful points.

It is probable that a combination of the above techniques will produce the best results. Observation on the spot and interviews with the job holder and his superior are generally regarded as essential. The analyst must, however, be able to conduct these interviews as speedily as possible to minimise the time people are away from their normal duties.

3. *Collation of Data*

The analyst should now edit the notes made during the interviews, separating the important information from the irrelevant and discarding statements of opinion as opposed to fact.

To facilitate the preparation of the draft job description the data should be recorded under the various specified headings, such as 'basic function', 'duties and responsibilities', etc.

A draft job description should now be written and discussed with the job holder and his superior to ensure that there are no omissions and that the job has been fully and accurately described. The successful completion of this stage which involves full consultation with those affected should facilitate their ready agreement to the use of the job description for the purposes previously outlined.

4. *Preparation of Job Description*

The final stage is, of course, the writing of the job description, and the use of a standard format and style facilitates the general use of job descriptions throughout an organisation. A description should:

(a) give a clear, concise and readily understood picture of the whole job;

(b) describe in sufficient detail each of the main duties and responsibilities;

(c) be in a crisp style, omitting all unnecessary words, each sentence starting preferably with a verb;

(d) indicate the degrees of direction received and supervision given;

(e) where an analytical scheme is being used, the job description will relate to the factors and sub-factors being used.

A job description is not intended to catalogue all duties involved with the result that an employee would feel justified in declining to perform any work not included in the description. It should be regarded as an outline of the minimum requirements of the job, thus preserving flexibility of operations.

The example on the following page of a general job description may serve to illustrate the principles already discussed.

We have already mentioned that the preparation of job descriptions is a very lengthy process. The maximum use should therefore be made of the descriptions, which have been produced at a considerable cost to the company. If rarely used, a job description becomes regarded as just another piece of paper which soon becomes out of date. To get the best value from them it should be borne in mind that:

1. A highly competent analyst should be employed.
2. Descriptions must be kept up to date.
3. They should be regularly used for the purposes described in this book.
4. Departmental supervisors should have ready access to descriptions for their people, as should the job holders themselves.
5. Descriptions should not be used so rigidly that, for example, operations are paralysed because workers refuse to carry out tasks which are not included in the job description. Like most instructions, they should be regarded as a guide to action.
6. Descriptions should not be so detailed and complicated that the key duties become obscured.

JOB DESCRIPTION

Job Title: Production Supervisor

1.	*Basic Function*	Supervised assigned factory production lines (3 in number) to ensure specified production requirements are met.
2.	*Reports to*	Production Manager.

3. *Major Responsibilities*

(a) Organise:

production lines (allocation of personnel, etc.) in conjunction with chargehands to ensure that products are manufactured according to schedule as directed by Production Manager;

meal stops and breaks to fit production schedule;

stops for machinery correction, maintenance or repair in conjunction with engineering department (in case of breakdown on line, to call in factory engineer immediately).

(b) Supervise:

all employees on production lines (discipline, absence, etc.) in conjunction with chargehands;

daily starting-up procedure and sterilisation of machinery after shut-down of lines at end of day;

safety of operations;

training of chargehands, leading hands and operatives;

housekeeping in production.

(c) Check:

specifications of products and the correct use of ingredientss logs of line speeds prepared daily by chargehands;

production output figures and reconcile daily with Depot;

raw material issue and reconcile weekly with Store; Department.

4. *Supervise*

(a) Directly:
3 chargehands.

(b) Indirectly:
6 leading hands
60 operatives.

5. *Co-ordination with*

Laboratory (specifications of products)
Stores chargehand (issue of materials)
Depot chargehand (production stock checks)
Office Manager (wages queries for staff)
Personnel Dept. (recruitment, staff welfare)

6. *Limits of Authority*

May stop production line of own accord (for machinery correction, maintenance or repair) provided stoppage is for reasonable time (less than half an hour).

May stop production line to fit in meal breaks.

May give limited time off to employees, in accordance with personnel procedures.

7. *Hours of Work* Monday to Friday 8 a.m. – 5 p.m. daily.

8. *Education/Experience* Preferably GCE level with technical bias: at least one year's experience on production lines.

Appendix II

CLASSIFICATION METHOD

A. Secretarial Grading Schedule

Level 1. Is required to be a skilled shorthand writer and/or machine transcriber and typist, able to deal with a quite varied and/or fairly technical vocabulary.

Deals in a limited manner with problems and/or people without reference to the manager, but is required to refer most things to him, dealing only with simple company routines in his absence.

Filters telephone calls and uses judgment in making appointments.

Organises straightforward subject filing restricted to main activities and correspondence, maintains straightforward departmental records.

Level 2. Is required to be a skilled shorthand writer and/or machine transcriber and typist, and deals with a varied and/or technical vocabulary.

Deals mainly with middle management, has occasional though limited contact with senior company executives. Is required to undertake routine correspondence herself.

Filters telephone calls and enquiries, exercises judgment in making appointments, and deals in a limited manner with problems and/or people without reference to the manager.

Deals with a fairly wide range of subject filing and correspondence, maintaining such work and staff records that are necessary—sometimes involving simple mathematical calculations.

Level 3. Capable of dealing with a variety of problems and/or people without reference to the manager. Undertakes some routine correspondence herself. Exercises judgment in making appointments, and filters telephone calls and answers enquiries.

Deals with complex files of correspondence and reports covering many subjects.

Has some contact with company executives at highest level and with important visitors, including overseas visitors. Deals widely with people at company middle management level.

Must be highly proficient in shorthand or machine transcribing and skilled in touch-typing; able to deal with a varied and technical vocabulary.

Maintains whatever records are necessary for office use.

Level 4. Has frequent contact with senior company executives and with important visitors including high-ranking overseas visitors. May arrange and sometimes take part in social activities for visitors.

Deals with complex files of correspondence and reports covering many subjects. Undertakes some correspondence herself; filters telephone calls and enquiries, exercises judgment in arranging appointments, and deals with a variety of problems and/or people without reference to the manager.

Is required to be highly proficient in shorthand or machine transcribing and touch-typing; able to cope with a very varied and, if necessary, technical vocabulary.

Maintains whatever records are necessary for office use.

81

B. An Example of Grade Descriptions for Technical Personnel

Level 1.   Work consisting mainly of routine activities under supervision and demanding only a small degree of initiative. Normally carried out by technicians without university or equivalent qualifications, but with sufficient experience to undertake simple technical assignments with minimum instruction. Newly qualified graduates will be placed in this grade while undergoing training for Level 2 jobs.

Level 2.   Work partly of a routine nature, but otherwise demanding judgment and analysis and carried out with a moderate amount of supervision by senior ranking technicians or supervisors, but may in turn involve the direction of the work of others. Work demands adequate experience in a particular field or, alternatively, a university degree or an equivalent qualification with sufficient practical experience.

Level 3.   Work involving the exercise of initiative and judgment with very little direct supervision, and demanding the ability to analyse problems and to devise suitable techniques for their solution. Work requires experience in the particular field of activity, possibly involving access to confidential information.

Level 4.   Work carried out by an expert in a major technical or specialised scientific field. Responsible only to higher supervision for development and experimental work or production control. May be subject to general guidance from Level 5 technicians or higher supervision. Work requires still more experience than Level 3 in the particular field of activity and will probably involve the possession of, or access to, highly confidential information.

Level 5.   Work carried out by scientists and technicians of outstanding ability and value to the company.

INSTITUTE OF OFFICE MANAGEMENT'S GRADING SCHEME

Level	Definition	Example
A	Tasks which require no previous clerical experience; each individual task is allotted, and is either very simple or closely directed.	(i) messenger work (ii) simpler forms of sorting.
B	Tasks which, because of their simplicity, are carried out in accordance with a limited number of well-defined rules after a comparatively short period of training (a few weeks); these tasks are closely directed and checked, and are carried out in a daily routine covered by a time-table and subject to short period control.	(i) simple copying work (ii) straight-forward adding operations using an adding machine.
C	Tasks which are of a routine character and follow well defined rules, but which require either a reasonable degree of experience or a special aptitude for the task, and which are carried out according to a daily routine covered by a time-table and subject to short period control.	(i) simple ledger machine operation. (ii) checking of B grade work.
D	Tasks which require considerable experience but only a very limited degree of initiative, and which are carried out according to a predetermined procedure and precise rules; the tasks are carried out according to a daily routine which varies but not sufficiently to necessitate any considerable direction.	(i) shorthand-typing of non-routine correspondence. (ii) certifying straight-forward purchase invoices by reference to orders and dockets for incoming goods.
E	Tasks which require a significant, but not extensive, measure of discretion, and initiative, or which require a specialised knowledge and individual responsibility for the work.	(i) group supervision of routine work (ii) dealing with queries of a non-routine character.
F	Tasks which necessitate exercising an extensive measure of responsibility and judgment or the application of a professional technique (legal, accounting, statistical, engineering).	(i) section supervision (ii) acting in close liaison with the management.

SAMPLE PREDETERMINED POINTS
ASSESSMENT TABLE

The table of points given below is one which has been used widely
in industry for the evaluation of manual jobs. It analyses base rate
considerations under four main heads and allocates points to clearly
defined job characteristics under each head. The relative value of
each of these main heads is not equal, and they were therefore
weighted by allocating a different points value to each characteristic.
It is common practice to break down ranges of points for each
characteristic into pre-defined levels, as shown in Appendix V.
In certain firms or industries with, for example, extremely heavy
work under poor conditions, it has been found necessary to alter
this weighting.

The total number of maximum variable points allocated to these
characteristics is 179, to which a datum of 100 is added, making a
possible total of 279 points for any one job. The points for each
characteristic and the total points for main heads and their respective
weightings are as shown on the table overleaf:

		Points for Characteristic	Total Maximum Points for each Main Head	Total Maximum Main Head Points as a % of 279
A.	*Acquired Skills and Knowledge*		88	32%
1.	Training and previous experience	40		
2.	General reasoning ability	23		
3.	Complexity of process	11		
4.	Dexterity and motor accuracy	14		
B.	*Responsibilities and Mental Requirements*		45	16%
1.	Responsibility for material or equipment	16		
2.	Effect on other operations	8		
3.	Attention needed to orders	12		
4.	Alertness to details	4		
5.	Monotony	5		
C.	*Physical Requirements*		15	5%
1.	Abnormal position	5		
2.	Abnormal effort	10		
D.	*Conditions of Work*		31	11%
1.	Disagreeableness	8		
2.	Danger	23		
	DATUM	100	100	36%
			279	100%

POINTS EVALUATION: THE TEXAS INSTRUMENTS' PLAN FOR MANUAL EMPLOYEES

Jobs are analysed under a maximum of fourteen factors, grouped under the following main heads:

skill
effort
responsibility
job conditions

Each factor is broken down into levels or degrees and these, together with the factor itself, are precisely defined. An example of how this operates in practice is as follows:

Factor: Experience

Experience is the measure of time ideally required by an individual with the specified education or trade knowledge to learn to perform satisfactorily the particular job being evaluated.

The measure of time should include *only* the actual job training required on the work to be performed plus any *necessary* experience on related work. Ideal training conditions are assumed where the variety and complexity of the work are so controlled that the individual spends only the minimum amount of time required to learn each phase of the work satisfactorily. No time is to be allowed beyond the bare minimum which is required for satisfactory performance. Thus repetitive experience beyond these *assumed ideal minimums* is not to be allowed. Also, only experience which is truly cumulative in its application to the job is to be credited.

The following guide should be applied when evaluating the factor *experience*:

(a) full credit for work in the grade or in the grade directly below;
(b) approximately 30% credit for lesser, but directly related experience (but not more than a maximum of about four years' credit);
(c) approximately 25% for other somewhat related experience (but not more than a maximum of about two years' credit).

1st *degree*: requires a short period of training on work to be performed or on directly related work not exceeding a total of three months.
2nd *degree*: over three months, up to one year.
3rd *degree*: over one year, up to three years.
4th *degree*: over three years, up to five years.
5th *degree*: over five years, up to eight years.
6th *degree*: over eight years, up to eleven years.

Experience degrees beyond 6th must be supervisory or very complex jobs of varied responsibilities. No more than three years allowed for each distinct phase requirement.

7th *degree*: over eleven years, up to fourteen years.
8th *degree*: over fourteen years, up to seventeen years.
9th *degree*: over seventeen years, up to twenty years.

Factor: Responsibility for Material or Product
This factor appraises the responsibility of an individual for avoiding loss to the organisation through waste or loss of raw material or product. The loss being evaluated is that which could reasonably result from any one failure to exercise due care, or any one series of incidents up to the point where they would be detected. Consider value of labour as well as material and also the possibility of salvage (use probable net loss).

In evaluating office and technical jobs, the above meaning is extended to include any monetary losses which might occur through inadequate care in purchasing, improper design of new products, clerical errors, inefficient operation due to inadequate planning, introduction of inadequate accounting or other procedures, or inadequate handling of any other functions which affect cost.

In appraising monetary responsibility for any specific job, consider double checks which are made on the work. The more the work is subject to checking, the less individual responsibility becomes.

1st degree: probable loss seldom over £5.
2nd degree: probable loss may exceed £5   but would seldom exceed £75.
3rd degree: probable loss may exceed £75   but would seldom exceed £150.
4th degree: probable loss may exceed £150   but would seldom exceed £300.
5th degree: probable loss may exceed £300   but would seldom exceed £1,500.
6th degree: probable loss may exceed £1,500   but would seldom exceed £5,000.
7th degree: probable loss may exceed £5,000   but would seldom exceed £7,500.
8th degree: probable loss may exceed £7,500   but would seldom exceed £15,000.
9th degree: probable loss may exceed £15,000   but would seldom exceed £35,000.
10th degree: probable loss may exceed £35,000   but would seldom exceed £70,000.
11th degree: probable loss may exceed £70,000   but would seldom exceed £140,000.

A points score for each factor is assessed according to the degree that each factor is present in the job according to the following schedule:

JOB FACTOR	DEGREE									
	1	2	3	4	5	6	7	8	9	10 Etc
Skill										
1. Education	14	28	42	56	70	84	98			
2. Experience	22	44	66	88	110	132	154			
3. Initiative, Ingenuity and Judgment	14	28	42	56	70	84	98	112	126	140
Effort										
4. Physical demand	10	20	30	40	50					
5. Mental or Visual demand (intensity)	5	10	15	20	25	30	35	40		
Responsibility										
6. Responsibility for Equipment or Process	5	10	15	20	25	30	35			
7. Responsibility for Material or Product	5	10	15	20	25	30	35	40	45	
8. Responsibility for Safety of others	5	10	15	20	25	30	35			
9. Responsibility for Work of others	5	10	15	20	25	30	35	40	45	
Job Conditions										
10. Working conditions	10	20	30	40	50					
11. Unavoidable hazards	5	10	15	20	25					

POINTS EVALUATION: AN EXAMPLE OF A PLAN FOR CLERICAL EMPLOYEES

FACTORS OF JOB EVALUATION

1. Educational requirements
2. Experience preferred
3. Complexity of duties
4. Responsibility for errors
5. Responsibility for contacts
6. Responsibility for confidential data
7. Manual dexterity—Visual attention—Mental concentration
8. Working conditions

When included as a requirement for any position:
9. Language ability

When supervision is an established function in the position:
10. Type of supervision
11. Extent of supervision

All factors are defined and are broken down into levels or degrees, and examples of two factor breakdowns are shown below.

1. *Education*

   This factor appraises the basic knowledge (however it may have been acquired) which the job requires as a background for training, preliminary to qualifying for the job. This basic knowledge may be acquired by formal education, outside study or on-the-job learning, depending on the nature of the position being rated. For ease in rating, the several degrees are expressed in terms of formal education.

   1st degree: mental alertness and adaptability to office routines. No specific knowledge required to perform the work other than the ability to read, write and do simple computations. Educational level of at least the minimum requirement established for employment.

   2nd degree: knowledge of business practice, e.g. stenography, operation of specialised office equipment such as book keeping, tabulating machine, simple blueprint reading, however acquired; or knowledge of operations or processes which require some specialised training.

   3rd degree: specialised knowledge in a field such as cost account, statistics, drawing office methods, or knowledge of operations and processes which require extended specialised training in fields such as chemistry, physics, metallurgy, electricity, company policies. Equivalent to a qualification obtained on completion of at least 3 years' part-time study.

4th degree: technical knowledge of a recognised profession such as engineering, accounting, finance or business administration, however acquired. Equivalent to a university degree.

5th degree: advanced technical knowledge in a recognised profession, obtainable usually only through one or two years of post-graduate work. Equivalent to Ph.D.

3. *Complexity of Duties*

This factor appraises the complexity of the work, the degree of independent action, the extent to which the duties are standardised, the judgment and planning required, the type of decisions made, and the creative effort required in devising ways of doing the job.

1st degree: simple routine, repetitive duties where the employee is told what to do at frequent intervals. Few decisions are necessary, and they require little individual judgment, usually because the work is either done under immediate supervision or involves little choice as to how to do it.

2nd degree: routine repetitive duties where the employee works from detailed instructions, makes minor decisions as to obvious errors, simple checking of work, when to ask for assistance. These decisions involve some judgment but the standardisation of the duties limits the planning and independent action to minor decisions not difficult to make since the choices are limited.

3rd degree: somewhat repetitive duties where the employee works from standard practice or generally understood methods of procedures which involve planning and performing several procedures. The sequence of steps usually will be determined by the employee on the basis of previous practice. Make decisions as to how and when the duties are to be performed. These decisions involve judgment to analyse facts in situations, plan work, determine what action should be taken within the limits of standard procedures, check work.

4th degree: difficult work where the employee works independently towards specific results. Plan and perform a sequence of procedures requiring a general knowledge of company policies and procedures and their application to cases not previously covered. Considerable ingenuity and judgment are required to diagnose and remedy trouble, devise methods, modify or adapt standard procedures to meet new conditions, make decisions based on policy and previous practice.

5th degree: complex and unusual work where the employee deals with new or constantly changing problems where there is little accepted method of procedure. Plan, lay out and perform a sequence of procedures involving creative effort. High degree of ingenuity and judgment are required to interpret results, plan work, deal with factors not easily evaluated, make decisions based on conclusions for which there is little precedent.

Points scores for each job are calculated by assessing the job under each of the factor headings and defining the appropriate level. The rating schedule and grades by point ranges are shown on following page.

PAGE	REF
90	4TH DEGREE
89	3RD /4TH
83	F
52	3/4
27	
9	4TH

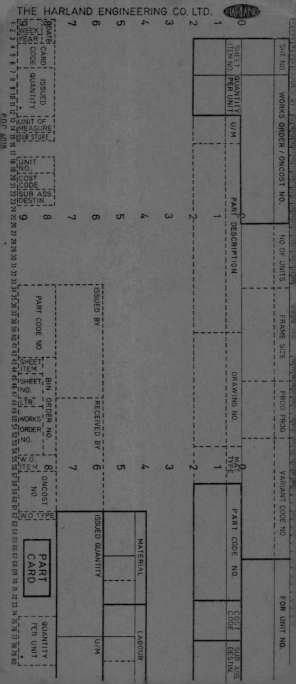

Job Rating Plan

Factors	1st degree	2nd degree	3rd degree	4th degree	5th degree
1. Education	15	30	45	60	75
2. Experience	15	30	45	60	75
3. Complexity of duties	15	30	45	60	75
4. Responsibility for errors	5	10	20	40	60
5. Responsibility for contacts with others	5	10	20	40	60
6. Responsibility for confidential data ..	5	10	15	20	25
7. Manual dexterity—Visual attention—Mental concentration ..	5	10	15	20	25
8. Working conditions	5	10	15	—	—
factors to be added for bilingual jobs only: 9. Languages	15	30	45	—	—
factors to be added for supervisory jobs only: 10. Type of supervision	5	10	20	40	60
11. Extent of supervision	5	10	20	40	60

Grades by Point Ranges

Grade	Point range
1	100
2	105–130
3	135–160
4	165–190
5	195–220
6	225–250
7	255–280
8	285–310
9	315–350
10	355–390
11	395–445
12	450–500

APPENDIX VII

DIRECT CONSENSUS METHOD
(ASSOCIATED INDUSTRIAL CONSULTANTS)

The direct consensus method of job evaluation is one which uses as a basis the comparison of jobs taken in pairs. The evaluation can also include the use of a factor plan suited to the particular circumstances of the organisation concerned. The marks available within a series of factors are not imposed. Instead all the interested parties combine to produce both the rank orders and the factor weights, so that the results are readily acceptable. And, finally, all the data processing—which includes the wage or salary analysis and the production of the evaluation results—is done automatically on the computer.

Compared to the point factor method, much less time is required to complete the evaluation, and the results and relevant costs are available as soon as this has been accepted.

Procedure

1. A sample of jobs which should be representative of all the types of work in the population of jobs is selected. The number of jobs chosen must be a prime number between 23 and 43.

2. Brief job descriptions of the sample jobs are prepared with the help of the job holders. Job descriptions for the remaining jobs in the population are required later in the job evaluation exercise.

3. Pre-printed ranking forms which compare each job in the sample with all the other jobs are available, and the job titles are typed on these forms ready for ranking.

4. A panel of judges, up to fifteen in number, is selected to represent all interested parties. For the standard number of jobs there is a preferred number of judges, and the distribution of the forms between the judges is such that all judges mark the same fraction of the total number of comparisons. The marking consistency of each judge can also be checked.

5. Each judge is presented with the forms containing the pairs of jobs, and is asked to prefer one job in each pair on the basis of overall worth. He indicates the preferred job by

inserting a tick (✓) against it. A tie may be awarded in the case of jobs of apparently equal worth, and, in such cases, a cross is placed against each job. When all the forms have been satisfactorily marked, the overall order and degree of agreement between the judges will be produced by the computer. (On the football league basis of win=2, draw=1, loss=0.)

6. The computer produces:
   (a) the overall rank order;
   (b) the degree of agreement among the judges;
   (c) the jobs about which there was the greatest disagreement.
   An example of a matrix is given at the end of this Appendix.

   Where the judges have exhibited strong preferences for a single job or group of jobs, very obvious gaps may appear in the computer print-out. These gaps can be used as a guide to the choice of grade boundaries, and the jobs can be grouped into grades. The remaining jobs of the population should be slotted into the proposed grade structure.

   This basic approach is simple and quick, and requires only the allocation of grades and rates of pay to enable the proposals to be costed using the wage analysis computer programme.

7. The preparation of a factor plan. In some organisations it may be advisable to ask the judges to justify their decisions by comparing jobs within clearly defined factors as well as on the basis of overall job worth. In this case a list of factors, preferably not more than six in number, should be chosen. These factors should be defined unambiguously, and should be mutually independent. Factor forms are then attached to the basic paired comparison forms and the judges are asked to compare jobs in pairs within each factor and on the basis of overall worth. The computer then establishes a rank order within each factor, and calculates factor weights which must generate the initial rank order.

8. Development of a wage structure. Using the overall rank order of sample jobs, an appropriate number of jobs is chosen. The jobs contained in each grade will serve to establish its characteristics.

   Concise job descriptions can now be prepared for the remaining jobs based on the qualifications defined by the factor plan. The evaluation committee can then use these descriptions to place as many jobs as can be agreed (usually 80%) into appropriate grades. Jobs about which the judges disagree are evaluated using the factor plan to determine their positions relative to the original sample of jobs. This final rank order is then used to decide on which side of the grade boundaries they fall.

9. Determination of wage or salary levels for individual grades. Wage levels are then chosen, using the computer to check the effect on individuals and on overall costs. Modifications to the grade contents and wage levels can be easily made so that an equitable basis for the wage structure negotiations can be produced.

Conclusion

The method of job evaluation described has been developed primarily to reduce the time and effort required in making large-scale job evaluations. It is simple, direct and open. It helps to provide a secure foundation on which to build a wage system which is satisfactory to all parties.

MATRIX SHOWING RESULTS OF COMPUTER ANALYSIS OF RANKING DECISIONS

```
23   I I 2 2 2 2 2 2 2 2 2 2 2 2 2 2 2 2 2 2 2 2 2 2 2 2 2 2 2 2 2 2 2 2 2 2
19   I I   I I 2 2 2 2 2 2 2 2 2 2 2 2 2 2 2 2 2 2 2 2 2 2 2 2 2 2 2 2 2 2 2 2
29     2 I 2   2 2 2 2 2 2 2 2 2 2 2 2 2 2 2 2 2 2 2 2 2 2 2 2 2 2 2 2 2 2 2 2
13     2   I   2 2 2 2 2 2 2 2 2 2 2 3 2 2 2 2 2 2 2 2 2 2 2 2 2 2 2 2 2 2 2 2
-01    I 2 2 I 2   2 2 2 2 2 2 2 2 2 2 2 2 2 2 2 2 2 2 2 2 2 2 2 2 2 2 2 2 2 2
08     I     I 2 2 2 2 2 2 I 2 2 2 2 2 2 2 2 2 2 2 2 2 2 2 2 2 2 2 2 2 2 2 2 2
24       2   I 2 2 2 2 2 2 2 2 2 2 2 2 2 2 2 2 2 2 2 2 2 2 2 2 2 2 2 2 2 2 2 2
-02        I 2 2 2 2 2 2 2 2 2 2 2 2 2 2 2 2 2 2 2 2 2 2 2 2 2 2 2 2 2 2 2 2 2
14         I I I 2 2 2   2 2 2 2 2 2 2 2 2 2 2 2 2 2 2 2 2 2 2 2 2 2 2 2 2 2 2
09         I I 2 2 2 2 2 2   2 2 2 2 2 2 2 2 2 2 2 2 2 2 2 2 2 2 2 2 2 2 2 2 2
-03    I       I I   2 2 2   2 2 2 2 2 2 2 2 2 2 2 2 2 2 2 2 2 2 2 2 2 2 2 2 2
25             2 I 2 2 2 2   2 2 2 2 2 2 2 2 2 2 2 2 2 2 2 2 2 2 2 2 2 2 2 2 2
30         I   2   I I   2 2 2 2 2 2 2 2 2 2 2 2 2 2 2 2 2 2 2 2 2 2 2 2 2 2 2
15             I I I I 2   2 I 2 2 2 2 2 2 2 2 2 2 2 2 2 2 2 2 2 2 2 2 2 2 2 2
34         2   2 I I I I I 2 2 2 2 2 2 2 2 2 2 2 2 2 2 2 2 2 2 2 2 2 2 2 2 2 2
-04            2 I I I   2 2 2 2 2 2 2 2 2 2 2 2 2 2 2 2 2 2 2 2 2 2 2 2 2 2 2
20           2 2   I 2 I   2 2 2 2 2 2 2 2 2 2 2 2 2 2 2 2 2 2 2 2 2 2 2 2 2 2
31         2       2 I 2 2 I   2 I 2 I 2 2 2 2 2 2 2 2 2 2 2 2 2 2 2 2 2 2 2 2
26         2         2   2 I     2 2 2 2 2 2 2 2 2 2 2 2 2 2 2 2 2 2 2 2 2 2 2
21             I       2 I   I 2   2 2 2 2 2 2 2 2 2 2 2 2 2 2 2 2 2 2 2 2 2 2
35                   I 2 2 I I I   2 2 2 2 2 2 2 2 2 2 2 2 2 2 2 2 2 2 2 2 2 2
16                   I I I I 2 2 2 2 2 2 2 2 2 2 2 2 2 2 2 2 2 2 2 2 2 2 2 2 2
-05            I     I I I I 2     2 2 2 2 2 2 2 2 2 2 2 2 2 2
10                   2 2   I I 2 I     2 2 2 2 2 2 2 2 2 2 2 2 2
36                 2     2   I I 2 I 2 2 2 2 2 2 2 2 2 2 2 2 2
17                   I I I     I 2 2 2 2 2 2 2 2 2 2
27                   2 2   2 I     2 2 2 2 2 2 2 2 2 2
32                 2 2 I 2 2 I 2   2 2 2 2 2 2 2 2 2 2
33                     2     I 2   I 2 2 2   I 2 2 2
-06                  I   2   I 2 2     2     2 2 2
-07                      2   I 2   I                 I
28                    I       I         2 2 2
22                    2 2 2 2 I         I 2
37                    I   2 2 2 I         I 2
11                      2 2     2 2 I I 2
18                          I       I I I I 2
12                          2                       I
```

Coefficient of agreement 0.92

GROUP NO. 2

ANALYTICAL GRADING (THE BRITISH BROADCASTING CORPORATION SYSTEM)

A. *Principles and Policy*

1. The method of grading all posts in the Corporation has its origin in the management's expressed policy:
   'to relate one job with another in a common grading structure'.
   This is done by defining the responsibilities and difficulty of posts at each level in every occupational group, and relating them to each other in a comprehensive grading scheme.

2. From this basic principle springs the idea of uniformity of approach as the base on which these common standards of fairness may most likely be achieved. It is also important to recognise that management is not thinking only of fair treatment as between individual members of staff but also between one area of work and another.

3. The further step is that the common standards of fairness are reflected in a common salary treatment which gives the same salary range to all staff on a given grade, regardless of the professional field in which they work.

4. In order to establish and operate such a uniform system of grading covering the whole Corporation, management decided that the task would be carried out centrally by a grading department. This is in parallel with centralised control of pay and conditions of service.

5. The basic principle having been laid down and the operational responsibility placed upon Grading Department, the problems of achieving fair grading and fair relativities had to be solved. In the BBC, not so much because of its size but rather because of the great diversity of functions and professions, these problems are not easy.

B. *The Method*

6. Any system developed in the Corporation, therefore, had

to aim at devising a method which would apply a common standard of measurement to all jobs. The method adopted and developed has been that of a form of analytical grading. This system has developed a series of common qualities or grading factors which provide a uniform basis of measurement of the comparative difficulties of all jobs, no matter how diverse the areas in which they operate and the functions which the holders perform.

7. The actual study of a job or category comprises two stages:
   (a) *job description:* this is a detailed statement of the functions required in a job and aims to record and communicate fully:
       (i)   the exact nature of the problems which must be solved as a post requirement,
       (ii) the authority vested in the post for taking decisions,
       (iii) supervision and other material assistance available;
   (b) *job analysis:* when the job description has been verified as correct (normally by the responsible departmental manager and post holder) the requirements of the job are analysed under factors:
       (i)   judgment,
       (ii) original thought,
       (iii) specialised knowledge and experience,
       (iv) man management,
       (v)   decisions.

8. *The five grading factors* are defined as follows:
   judgment
   The process of selecting a course of action by the analysis and appraisal of the merits and demerits of each of a number of courses, either specified or discerned. It is recognised that there are two elements involved, viz: the *complexity* of selection, and the uncertainty (*intangibility*) in making a choice.
   original thought
   The conception and formulation of new ideas, techniques, or methods, and the devising of modifications to existing ones.
   specialised knowledge and experience
   The specialised knowledge and/or experience necessary to arrive at a solution to problems.

man management
The ability to persuade people to adopt a particular course of action, or to extract from them a maximum potential contribution.
decisions
Decisions affecting BBC policy and the use of the BBC's resources, and involving accountability for:

money:	the allocation or use of the BBC's financial resources
facilities:	the allocation or use of the BBC's resources of equipment and property
staff:	the allocation, use, or treatment of the BBC's employees
air time:	the allocation or use of the BBC's transmission time in terms of programme content
public relations:	the information given to the public about the BBC's activities and policies.

9. *Five full grade levels* of *each* factor are defined. In any job the different factors may, of course, apply to a different degree. The overall grade of the job, however, *is the highest grade obtained in any one of the five factors*, provided that it relates to a regular and substantial part of the holder's required duties.

10. Intermediate grades provide for those posts which do not, for one reason or another, fully reflect a full grade level.

The system is fully documented in the book *Managerial and Professional Staff Grading*, by Joan Doulton and David Hay.

THE HAY-MSL EXECUTIVE JOB EVALUATION METHOD

Hay-MSL (a consultancy concern owned by Hay International (U.S.A.), and the M.S.L. Group (U.K.)) offer a system of job evaluation and combine it with external comparisons of total salary structures to establish market rates.

The key point about the system is the yardstick of measurement. Two principle measuring instruments are used in this system: Hay Guide Charts and Job Profiles.

The Guide Charts cover three principle areas:

1. *Input of know-how*
    The technical, scientific and professional knowledge, skill and experience required in the job, plus the managerial scope of the job in terms of planning, organising, evaluating, developing and co-ordinating, plus the human relations skills involved in influencing people.

2. *Output of accountability*
    The significance of the results to be achieved in the job in terms of freedom to act in pursuance of results, the value of resources controlled, and the degree of impact of the job on the organisation's objectives.

3. *Output of problem solving*
    The nature, depth, quality frequency of problems to be solved. The degree to which problems in the job involve creative, analytical, or merely repetitive thought processes.

Each job is rated in each separate area, and subsequently all jobs are compared in relation to their total ratings. When all jobs in an organisation are plotted on the charts, they thus illustrate in quantitative terms the job structure of the organisation.

The Job Profiles measure two relationships:

1. The relationship between input of know-how into the job, and the output of problem solving (advice) and accountability (active results) expected in the job. Input and output must be in proper relationship if a job is to be viable.

2. The relationship between the problem solving (advisory) content of jobs and the accountability content. A balance between 'think' and 'do' is established in each job, and between problem solving (think) jobs and accountability jobs in the total organisation.

TIME SPAN

The time span approach to the analysis and measurement of work, developed by Dr. Elliott Jaques, differs in a number of respects from other systems of job evaluation because, instead of considering all the human attributes and characteristics required to meet successfully the physical and mental demands of a job (e.g. skill, mental and physical requirements, responsibilities and working conditions), it fixes emphasis on two rather different aspects of the work situation.

Under normal conditions of employment, no one has absolute freedom of action. All activity is approved within certain limits, explicitly or implicitly, set by a superior and accepted as part of his job by the individual. Within the constraints which are inevitably present, the individual, in order to get his work done and achieve the results required, has to make decisions which involve the elements of choice. Work activities are therefore divided into elements that are:

prescribed (i.e. laid down so that there is no authorised choice)

and

discretionary (in that judgment and decision making are called for).

All work, even that which is described as purely routine, requires the exercise of some discretion, and no discretion can be exercised indefinitely without at some point being checked and reviewed by a superior.

The time span of a job is defined as 'the longest period of time which can elapse before a manager can decide that his subordinate has not been exercising marginal sub-standard discretion in balancing the pace and quality of his work'. Gross errors of judgment or flagrant mistakes (people are not authorised to be negligent) are normally readily and quickly perceived, but what are termed to be marginally sub-standard decisions would take longer to detect. However, a point in time is reached when the manager has to ask himself whether the quality of the judgments and decisions made is acceptable. For the individual, the longer the period of suspense, the greater are his feelings of anxiety and sense of responsibility.

The longer the organisation, *through the manager*, is prepared to allow the individual to commit its resources (including the deployment of his own time) without being able to ascertain whether the commitment has been effective, the higher will be considered the level of work in the role occupied.

Basically the procedure for time span measurement can be shown as a number of distinct steps, viz:

1. Discussions with the immediate manager of the person whose level of work is to be measured, in order to ascertain the means by which any sub-standard discretion exercised by the job holder would come to his attention. Also the immediate manager is accountable for knowing, or being able to discover, the kind of tasks he is assigning as authorised by his own manager. The essential objective of this analysis is to require the immediate manager to define the target completion times in the case of a multiple task role, or quality standards in the case of a single role, beyond which he would not be prepared to let his subordinate go without criticising him for sub-standard work.

2. Discussions with the job holder to obtain *his views* of the information above, and to compare this with (or supplement) the information obtained from the immediate manager. Should there be any variations, these must be resolved, if if necessary by reference to the next level of line manager.

3. Determine whether the job is 'multi-task' or 'single-task'. Tasks are defined as discrete and finite units of work which the subordinate must carry out. Distinction must be drawn between the physically delegated tasks and general responsibilities. In a single-task role the job holder never has more than one task to work on at a time, and he continues until he has completed it. A series of single tasks may be assigned with the instructions to complete them one at a time in a particular sequence. In a multi-task role a mixture of tasks is assigned. There is no particular order of tasks, and there is discretion exercised as to how and when the tasks should be completed.

4. If it is a multi-task role, ascertain the longest extended task, as the *level of work relates to the time span of the target completion time of the longest task.*

5. If it is a single-task role, ascertain the longest task or task

sequence, as the *level of work relates to the time span of the target completion time of the task or task sequence.*

6. Confirm that the immediate manager is authorised to delegate the level of the work being undertaken by the job holder. This is done by reference to the manager once removed from the job holder, and thus the time span measurement is authorised.

Payment is related to the level of work as reflected by the time span measurement.

In practice, time span is likely to be found more immediately useful for the measurement of general staff and managerial roles, although it can be applied equally to manual as to staff roles. Those who have had experience of its application have been impressed by the results obtained and the remarkable correlation which seems to exist between them and those derived from other systems of job evaluation. Furthermore, the absence of subjectivity covers the high degree of consistency in the results obtained by different people undertaking the analysis.

The above method is dealt with more fully in Elliott Jaques' books *Equitable Payment* and *Time Span Handbook.*

READING LIST

Note: The following list is supplementary to the reading of this book and is not intended as a comprehensive job evaluation bibliography. Any item out of print is available on loan to members from the BIM Library. A more detailed reading list on job evaluation is also available from the BIM Library.

BENGE, EUGENE J., *The Factor Comparison Method of Job Evaluation.* 12pp.

DOULTON, J. AND HAY, D., *Managerial and Professional Staff Grading.* Allen and Unwin for the Royal Institute of Public Administration, 1962. 141pp.

FOX, ALAN, *The Time-Span of Discretion Theory: An Appraisal.* Institute of Personnel Management, 1966. 30pp.

GOMBERG, WILLIAM, *A Labour Union Manual on Job Evaluation,* second edition. Labour Education Division, Roosevelt College, Chicago, 1948. 80pp.

INCOMES DATA SERVICES LIMITED, *Guide to Salary Surveys.* London, 1969. 32pp.

INSTITUTE OF OFFICE MANAGEMENT, THE, *Clerical Job Grading and Merit Rating.* 1960.

INSTITUTE OF OFFICE MANAGEMENT, THE, *Clerical Job Grading Schedule.* 1964.

INTERNATIONAL LABOUR OFFICE, *Job Evaluation.* Geneva, 1960. 146pp.

JAQUES, ELLIOTT, *Equitable Payment: A General Theory of Work, Differential Payment, and Individual Progress,* revised edition. Penguin Books, Harmondsworth, Middlesex, 1967. 382pp.

JAQUES, ELLIOTT, *Progression Handbook.* Heinemann, 1968. 72pp.

JAQUES, ELLIOTT, *Time-Span Handbook.* Heinemann, 1964. 133pp.

LYTLE, C. W., *Job Evaluation Methods,* second edition. Ronald Press, New York, 1954. 507pp.

McBEATH, G. AND RANDS, D. N., *Salary Administration,* second edition. Business Books Limited, 1969. 283pp.

MORRIS, J. WALKER, *Job Evaluation,* third edition, revised. Institute of Supervisory Management, Birmingham, 1968. 48pp.

NATIONAL BOARD FOR PRICES AND INCOMES, *Job Evaluation.* H.M.S.O., London, 1968. (Report No. 83.) 49pp.

NATIONAL BOARD FOR PRICES AND INCOMES, *Job Evaluation.* H.M.S.O., London, 1968. (Supplement to Report No. 83.) 65pp.

OTIS, JAY L. AND LEUKART, RICHARD H., *Job Evaluation: A Basis for Sound Wage Administration*, second edition. Prentice-Hall, New York, 1954. 532pp.

THOMASON, GEORGE F., *Personnel Manager's Guide to Job Evaluation.* Institute of Personnel Management, London, 1968. 49pp.

TRADES UNION CONGRESS, *An Outline of Job Evaluation and Merit Rating.* 1964. 20pp.

Articles in Periodicals

Industry Week, 8 August 1969, pp. 27-30
'Profile Method of Job Evaluation', by A. L. T. Taylor.
Management Today, July 1968, pp. 58-61
'How to Evaluate Jobs', by T. M. Husband.
Personnel and Training Management, September 1968, pp. 15-18
'Building a New Job Evaluation Structure', by Stanley Luckhurst.

GLOSSARY OF JOB EVALUATION DEFINITIONS

Basic rate: the rate paid for a job, before the addition of piecework, bonus earnings, special allowances, etc. (cf. *Job rate*).

Benchmark or *Key job:* a job selected for one or more of the following purposes:

    (a)   as a standard against which other jobs are assessed;

    (b)   as representing a particular grade of work;

    (c)   as a sample for remuneration surveys.

Category: a group of two or more jobs of like work in which the holders are readily interchangeable without further training.

Characteristic: see under *Factor.*

Degree: see under *Level.*

Factor or *Characteristic:* in an analytical method of job evaluation the main headings against which the jobs under review will be assessed.

Grade: a group of jobs for which it has been agreed to pay the same base rate.

Job: the total work (i.e. all the tasks) assigned to an individual by management.

Job analysis: the process of determining the tasks involved in, and the requirements of, a job.

Job description: a record under an appropriate job title of the conditions, tasks, responsibilities and organisational placing of a job, including specification of the skills required of the job holder in order satisfactorily to perform the tasks and responsibilities.

Job evaluation: the process of analysis and assessment of the relative content of jobs to place them in an acceptable rank order which can be used as a basis for a pay structure.

Job grading: the process of putting jobs into the appropriate grades.

Job rate: the rate to be paid for performance of all aspects of the job requirements. For example, in a piecework situation this equates to the basic plus the 'bonus' rate: in a high day rate plant this would equate to the basic rate. (cf. *Basic rate.*)

Key job: see under *Benchmark.*

Level or *Degree:* the amount of demand present in a job for a particular factor or sub-factor, using some form of scale.

Market groups: a family of jobs in which the recruitment qualifications overlap and amongst which employees can readily move by extending or adapting their skills.

Pay structure: the system of payments which are related to the jobs an employee carries out. For manual workers it is the monetary relationships between basic rates, or basic rates with the addition of job evaluated plus rates; for salaried employees it is the relationship between the pay ranges applicable to job grades.

Payment system: a generic term collectively referring to the various methods of payment, for instance, high day rate, measured day work, the various PBR systems, and so on.

Rank: the hierarchical relationship of one job to another.

Remuneration system: the sum of all the components which go to make up the gross pay an employee receives. Thus it consists of basic pay, merit or incentive payments, shift pay where applicable, and so on.

Sub-factor or Sub-characteristic: in an analytical method of job evaluation the recognisably different aspects of factors.

Task: a unit of work forming the whole or part of a job for which a specific result is required. In discussing time span the specific result is set against an explicit or implicit time limit.

Time span: the maximum period of time during which the use of discretion, excluding gross errors of judgment, is authorised and expected, without review of that discretion by a superior.

Weighting: the process of allocating relative significance to different factors used in job evaluation.

Work classification: the classification of work into groups of like activities, e.g. Transport, Engineering and Maintenance Services, or Accountancy, Industrial Engineering, etc.

DEFINITIONS OF METHODS OF JOB EVALUATION

A. NON-ANALYTICAL METHODS

1. *Job ranking*

   A job evaluation method that considers the relative importance of each job *as a whole* directly against all other jobs in the area under review.

2. *Job Classification/Grading*

   A job evaluation method whereby the whole jobs are compared against predetermined criteria in order to identify their appropriate place in a previously defined grading and/or pay structure.

B. ANALYTICAL METHODS

The essential feature of analytical methods of job evaluation is that instead of evaluating each job as a whole it is considered under a series of predetermined factors which can be applied to all the jobs under review.

1. *Analytical Grading*

   A job evaluation method combining in a single approach characteristics of the grading and factor assessment.

2. *Points Assessment*

   A job evaluation technique in which each factor used has a quantitative scale of points against which jobs are assessed.

3. *Factor Comparison*

   A job evaluation method whereby jobs are examined using a predetermined monetary scale for each factor.

4. *Profiling*

   This technique assesses jobs factor by factor in terms of four or five significant levels of difference. Weighting of factors is determined by paired comparison of a number of benchmark jobs, quantification of the individual assessments of these and a matching of the two sets of data.